Turkey File

A rising star and its place in the world

Alan F. Scott

ISBN: 1470082470
ISBN 13: 9781470082475

For Dilek

A critical listener and loving supporter

Contents

Author's Preface

When I first came to Turkey in 1995, I knew little about the country. In fact, that is not entirely true. As a New Zealander, I had grown up with stories of the Gallipoli campaign, that bloody sideshow of the First World War, which cost so many lives and achieved so little. Brought up in a church-going family, I was well versed in the scriptures and gospels, especially the epistles of Paul to the churches of ancient Christendom. As a student of a model English grammar school, I spent five years studying Latin and the achievements and culture of the Roman Empire. Being a reader, and having an interest in history, I knew, of course, of the Byzantine and Ottoman Empires. I had even heard of Mustafa Kemal Atatürk, and somewhere or other had come across the modern Turkish alphabet, a deceptively familiar yet not-quite-accessible version of our Latin-based one, with its peculiar accent marks and unexpected cedillas. My studies of 19th century European history had familiarised me with 'The Eastern Question' and 'The Sick Man of Europe', and my readings of Shakespeare had mixed ominous references to the 'heathen Turk' with the folk culture that embodied names like Genghis and Attila with a power of evil beyond the capacity of mere words.

Yet I had no concept of the country that is the modern Republic of Turkey. I had all these snippets of knowledge buzzing around in what I liked to think of as my world-view. But I had no unifying idea that they all occurred within the boundaries of that little known and little understood nation on the back-doorstep of Europe.

Perhaps it was to my advantage that I came from a country far from the fast lanes of geopolitics. There was no visible Turkish diaspora in New Zealand to imbue me with a prejudice against migrant workers.

My preconceptions were more deep-seated and subliminal, but none-theless real, being part of the cultural baggage I carried as an educated product of an Anglo/Euro-centric system and culture.

Almost from the moment the wheels of my British Airways Boeing hit the tarmac at Atatürk Airport, I found these cultural assumptions challenged in ways that I had never imagined. In the years since then, while making a life for myself as a teacher of English in Turkey, I have continued to benefit from the mind-expanding shocks and jolts that strike the foreigner in this much-misunderstood land.

I remember looking at an atlas, on first coming to Turkey. It was quite a good atlas, a reputable publication that I had bought while study-ing Geography at Auckland University. I still have it, in fact, and I have counted twenty-one pages on the British Isles, ten pages on the United States of America, and even little old New Zealand warrants a two-page spread. Interestingly, however, there is not one single page devoted to the modern Republic of Turkey, a country three times the size of New Zealand, or Great Britain, or Japan, and in population, second only to the united Germany among European nations.

It is a small thing, perhaps, and of no special significance. I've never been a fan of conspiracy theories. But again, I couldn't help being puz-zled when I learnt that the Turks celebrate 18 March as Victory Day in their Çanakkale War (which we know as the Gallipoli campaign). Hang on a minute! We (Anzacs etc) didn't even get there till 25 April! As educated adults, we need to feel confident that history has an objectiv-ity that places it above partisan politics and racial stereotypes, so how to account for this major disparity of dates? In fact, as I later learned, the Gallipoli landings were Plan B, made necessary because of the failure of Plan A. For the Turks, their success in turning back the Royal Navy from the Dardanelles was the more important part of the victory. For the British Empire, no doubt, that was a setback better consigned to the footnotes of history.

Historical events, dates and personages are one aspect of the con-struct of the world that we all carry with us. But there is another, less overt, perhaps more powerful force shaping our judgments of other peoples and races: the proverbial wisdom, folk knowledge and cultur-al assumptions that we inhale with the air of the society in which we grow up and receive our education. So Genghis Khan and Attila the

Hun have such a basic existence in the consciousness of Western minds that no knowledge of history is necessary to conjure up images of marauding barbaric hordes sweeping out of the Asian steppe, laying waste all in their path like an invasion of killer bees. When I learned that the principal of my school, a tall, distinguished-looking gentleman of scholarly bearing was called Genghis, it required in me a shift of mental gears. Hearing also that Attila was the name of that polite, hand-raising, homework-doing young lad in my year 9 class was a further surprise for which my Euro-centric upbringing had not prepared me.

I would like to share some of the experiences I have had since I first came to this surprising country, and some of the eye-opening knowledge that has come my way, bringing me to a better understanding of a place that has become my second home.

1

Where Are The Ancient Treasures of Turkey?

17 May 2009

Her çiçek bahçesinde
Her eser ülkesinde güzeldir

Every flower is beautiful in its own garden
Every work of art, in its own country

(PLAQUE ON THE WALL OF THE SELÇUK MUSEUM, TURKEY)

Another tourist season is beginning. Chartered planefuls of Brits, Russians, Germans, descend again on the resorts of Turkey: Kuşadası, Bodrum, Alanya . . . regale themselves with Efes Pilsen and breakfasts of bacon and eggs as they toast to unfashionable shades of pink in the unaccustomed heat of the Mediterranean and Aegean sun. Increasing numbers of them, lured by the foregoing pleasures, and relatively affordable property prices, purchase a slice of local real estate and return to the same villa year after year, or send their neighbours from back home.

For many foreign visitors, this is Turkey. But of course, there are other Turkeys, and many other reasons for visitors to come, no less in the

21st century than in the 13th For Christians there are places of pilgrimage in this nursery of early Christianity: the great church of St Sophia in Istanbul, the house of the Virgin Mary at Ephesus, St Peter's first church in ancient Antioch (modern Antakya) to name only three. For students of history, and those with a passing interest, this is one of the cradles of civilisation, its ancient land buried in layers of more long-gone peoples and empires than probably any other place on Earth: Hittite, Lydian, Lycian, Ionian, Roman, Seljuk . . .

So we visit the museums, the unearthed and reconstructed sites of ancient cities, and, if we have a modicum of imagination, we guess that even the grains of sand, on which we arrange our white plastic *şezlong,* are the eroded remains of palaces and bath houses, monuments and triumphal fountains of once-great empires. Perhaps, in the raptures of such imaginings, we pick up a fragment of white marble lapped by the waves at our feet, and secrete it in our pack to use as a paperweight in memory of our travels. What harm in that? Who could object?

I guess it's a question of scale. There must surely be a continuum of theft, from the accidental accumulation of clay or sand on the soles of my shoes accompanying me back home after my holiday – to the meticulously planned heist which removes a priceless Van Gogh or Monet from the wall of the Musee d'Orsay to grace someone's private art collection.

I paid another visit to the museum at Selçuk last summer. It's a small museum, but important in that the town of Selçuk is a popular base for exploring the ruins of the city of Ephesus, once capital of the ancient Aegean region of Asia Minor, and home of the early church to which St Paul addressed one of his famous epistles.

Among the important archaeological finds at Ephesus is the Parthian monument. The Parthians were a warlike race whose territory lay at the Eastern border of the Roman Empire. There were ongoing wars between the Romans and the Parthians involving victories on either side, but the Romans never succeeded in subduing them. The monument in question commemorated a victorious campaign undertaken by Roman forces against the Parthians during the reign of the Emperor Trajan in 116 CE, and was decorated with reliefs showing scenes from the wars. Some of the reliefs that once adorned the monument are displayed in the

Selçuk Museum – the majority, however, are in the Ephesus Museum in Vienna.

If this were a single event in which the priceless remains of an ancient civilisation had been removed from their original site to a museum abroad it would be serious enough. A strong case might be made for their return to Turkey. It is, however, just one instance of countless cases where ancient flowers have been removed from their natural garden to some public museum or private collection in another country. And, as we all know, there is safety in numbers. Why should I return my reliefs until they hand back their caryatids?

Just a short stroll down the road from the marble columns and friezes of Ephesus is the site of the fabled Temple of Artemis. Of course, as an important goddess in the Greek pantheon, Artemis had more than one temple built in her honour. But this was THE Temple of Artemis, one of the reasons for the fame of the city of Ephesus, and one of the Seven Wonders of the Ancient World. Sadly, visitors today will be disappointed if they expect to see more than orderly rows of foundation stones and a half-hearted reconstruction of an ancient column. Those from London especially could have saved themselves the airfare to Turkey, when a tube ride to Russell Square and a short walk to the British Museum would have enabled them to see more of the temple than can be seen in situ.

And for those Brits who read this book in time to save on the plane ticket, while you're at the British Museum, check out the statues and other remains from the Mausoleum of Halicarnassus, another of those legendary Seven Wonders. If you were expecting to see much of it during breaks away from the Bodrum nightclubs, you'd be better off ordering another Efes Pilsen.

Still, we can't blame only the Brits. I've already mentioned the Viennese, and in fact it was crusading Christian knights who originally dismantled most of the fabulous Mausoleum to build their castle defending the harbour at Bodrum. U.S. presidents would do well to check their history books before siding too readily with those medieval crusaders. On one of their sacred outings in 1204, they stopped off on their way to fight the Muslims in the Holy Land, and sacked the city of Constantinople. Some sources tell us that the sacking of the city and raping of the (Christian) inhabitants went on for three days, during Easter week! Sure the city was conquered by the Muslim Ottomans in

1453, but by then most of the riches of the St Sophia Cathedral and nearby imperial statuary had already been shipped off to Venice and Florence, where they can, so I'm told by reliable sources, be seen today.

But in spite of all this, many of us go to Turkey, and not just for the beaches. Of course, it is still a rich storehouse of remains of ancient cultures. What about Troy? You've seen the movie, and you know the Greeks sailed across the Aegean to recapture the beautiful Helen. Again, sadly, visitors to Troy are likely to be disappointed. A certain Heinrich Schliemann, 19th century German archaeologist, and his wife, who apparently rejoiced in the delightfully classical name of Sophia Engastromenos, with the connivance of a corrupt Ottoman official, spirited away the legendary treasures of Troy.

Never mind, you may think. Anyway, I was going to Berlin to check out the Pergamum Museum, which, as you know, was purpose-built to exhibit the altars, statues and friezes taken from the site of ancient Pergamum, near the town of Bergama in modern Turkey. I can kill two birds with the Berlin stone, you may think. But again, you will be disappointed. The Trojan treasures apparently disappeared from Berlin in 1945, and their whereabouts remained a mystery until 1993, when the Pushkin Museum in Moscow announced that they were, in fact, in safe-keeping, stored in their basement, and would shortly go on display. Can making off with already previously made-off-with artefacts be considered a crime? Working on the mathematical principle of two negatives making a positive, one might plead not.

Well, I could go on and tell you more about the whereabouts of the treasures of ancient Turkey. I've barely touched on the riches of Constantinople and Pergamum, now securely housed elsewhere, and I haven't even mentioned Sardis, a once grand city at the western end of the trade route linking Mesopotamia to the Aegean region, capital of the proverbial Lydian King Croesus – but I think you get the picture. Luckily for Turkey and the rest of us who love to travel, the best efforts of treasure-hunters and pillagers from the West have as yet been unable to denude Turkey of the wealth of ancient cultures to be found within its borders. Drop a spade into the ground anywhere in Istanbul, or elsewhere in the country, and the chances are you'll uncover something of deep historical significance. It's certainly worth a visit – and not just to Kuşadası!

2

Beyond the Black Stump -
The 'Otherness' of Turkey

18 June 2009

In 2001 there was a UEFA Cup football match in Istanbul between the local club Fenerbahçe, and a Greek team from Athens, Panathinaikos. The Greek team were defeated, and their supporters received a lot of negative publicity for the damage caused after the match to the Fenerbahçe stadium. I remember seeing a photograph in a local newspaper of a group of Fenerbahçe supporters who, during the course of the match, delighted in waving a large banner on which was emblazoned the inflammatory message: 'Welcome to Istanbul – ours since 1453!'

This date, 1453, is sometimes taken by historians as marking the end of the Middle Ages – it is arguably of more international significance than the year (1483) when Henry Tudor defeated the Yorkist usurper, Richard III, in a relatively minor island state on the western outskirts of Europe, as my school textbook suggested.

Not that it's a year much celebrated outside of Turkey. This year, 29 May marked the 556th anniversary of the Ottoman conquest of Constantinople – so you'd have to think that the likelihood of the Turks packing their bags and heading back to Central Asia where they came from is decreasing with the passing years. Nevertheless, they still seem to have some difficulty in getting themselves accepted as bona fide members of the Europe Club.

The most obvious problem is that the Turks are overwhelmingly Muslim, and the mental baggage we Westerners inherited from our Crusader ancestors, inclines most of us to view Muslims with suspicion at the very least. But it's not just that. There's a serious dichotomy in the prevailing Western view of the part of the world currently called the Republic of Turkey, which goes back beyond the arrival of marauding hordes from the steppes of Asia.

Constantinople, and the Byzantine Empire of which it was the capital city, was 'Christian', and therefore the fall of the city was a terrible blow struck against Christendom by the forces of Islam. John Julius Norwich, in his 'History of Byzantium', postulates that, had it not been for the persistence of the Eastern Roman Empire for a thousand years after the fall of Rome, the whole of Europe could well have been overrun, and we would see nothing strange about trotting off to the local mosque five times a day at the call of the muezzin.

On the other hand, the Byzantine Empire, and hence Constantinople, were not 'real' Christians. They were portrayed in Europe as heretics and schismatics who did not belong to the 'true' church (namely, the church of Rome). That was undoubtedly one reason medieval western Christendom would not send aid to their fellow Christians against the threat of militant Islam. It's also likely that they knew the cause was hopeless and preferred to stay on the sidelines.

When Constantine moved the capital of the Roman Empire to Constantinople in 330 CE, the city was, by definition, the centre of an empire that was unquestionably European. However, as the city of Rome lost its imperial power and became dependent for its prestige on the rise of Christianity and its chief Bishops (read 'Popes', if you prefer), it became necessary to emphasise the 'otherness' of Constantinople, which retained its temporal power (along with powerful religious influence) for centuries after the fall of the Western Roman Empire.

This concept of 'otherness' was later solidified in Western thinking by the adoption of the term 'Byzantine' to describe the Roman Empire in the east that survived after the fall of the Western Roman Empire to the barbarians in the 5th century. In fact, the word 'Byzantine', was not used by those people to describe themselves, and according to the Merriam-Webster Dictionary, was first used by European historians in the mid-17th century.

We may account for the adoption of this term by hypothesising that classical scholars in succeeding centuries were enamoured of the (pagan) Roman Empire which they saw as epitomising all the virtues to which they aspired as sons of a new world empire. Naturally they were reluctant to accept that the direct heirs of this great classical empire were the decadent, heretical, pseudo-Christians of the eastern Mediterranean.

During the Middle Ages, crusades were sent from Western Europe to free the so-called Holy Land from the yoke of the Islamic Turks, despite the fact that there was a Christian power on the doorstep of those holy places. One can easily imagine that the whole Crusade business was a ploy by the Bishops of Rome to unite western Christendom against a common enemy in an attempt to regain the temporal power that had been lost with the fall of Rome to the barbarians (which power, we may assume, they greatly envied their eastern brothers). The fact that these western 'Crusaders' did not consider the Eastern Christians co-religionists is emphasised by the sack of Constantinople by forces of the Fourth Crusade in 1204.

Returning to an earlier point (Constantinople as a disaster for Christendom as a whole), western sources of dubious historical veracity have subsequently tried to assert kinship with the brave defenders of the city by a) reminding us that there were Genoese and Venetians (the right kind of Christians) among the defenders and b) asserting that the desperate defenders held ecumenical services of communion in the cathedral of St Sophia as the axe began to fall. We gather that the errant Easterners were beginning to see the light, though sadly for them, it was too little, too late.

Linking to an issue that I will discuss in a later chapter, in the 19th century, European interests, especially Great Britain, were encouraging the Greek-speaking peoples of the Aegean to form a nationalist consciousness and rebel against the Ottoman Empire. The emergence of the modern nation-state of Greece in 1832 was made possible only with major support from the British and French fleets of the day. This encouragement culminated in an invasion of Western Anatolia by a mainland Greek military force under the aegis of the victorious Allies at the end of the 1st World War.

The 'megali idea', on which this invasion was based, was the concept of the recreation of a semi-mythical Greek empire centred on the Aegean. Of course, for the Greeks, this dream could never be fulfilled without the inclusion of the former imperial and religious capital of Constantinopolis – something which, one suspects, the Allies had no intention of allowing. The city straddling the Bosporus Straits, and bridging the continents of Europe and Asia, had too much geo-political significance to be given over to what could only ever be a minor player in world politics. It is fairly clear that the 'megali idea', and the encouragement of Greek nationalism by the western powers, was primarily aimed at disempowering and dismantling the Ottoman Empire, and creating a puppet Greek state in the strategic zone of the eastern Mediterranean.

It's a complex history, made more complex after the conquest of Constantinople by the Muslim Ottomans in 1453 and the city's status as capital of their Islamic empire for nearly five hundred years. The Western point-of-view seems to have always struggled to come to grips with reality in this part of the world. The invention of the word 'Byzantine' to name the Eastern Roman Empire that survived for a thousand years after the fall of Rome is just one example of this.

The refusal of history to conform to Western plans was further confirmed when, against all expectations, a blond, blue-eyed genius from Salonika led the Turkish rump of the Ottoman Empire to military and political success in the establishment of the modern Republic of Turkey.

After 556 years, 29 May is still a big one for Turks – and a thorn in the side of visiting football teams from Athens.

3

Cyprus - What are the Turks doing there anyway?

19 July 2009

No one in the world recognises the Turkish Republic of Northern Cyprus except Turkey, and, one must suppose, the people who actually live there, but we can't count them, because no one recognises them, except Turkey, and the people who ... Well, clearly this isn't getting us anywhere! We'll need to try starting somewhere else.

One of my first expeditions out of Istanbul was with a busload of Turkish High School students and teachers. It was an educational trip, for me, perhaps, more than the students. We visited the battlefields and cemeteries of Gallipoli, the excavations of ancient Troy, and the ruins of ancient Assos scattered through the rustic village of Behramkale.

The hill rising above the blue waters of the Aegean commands an impressive view over the sea and the islands so steeped in history and beloved of modern sun-seeking tourists.

'What's that island?' I asked one of my Turkish colleagues, pointing to a largish landmass rising from the sea about ten kilometres away.

'Well, we call it Midilli', was the reply, 'but Europeans know it as Lesbos – it's a Greek Island.' A quick check of Google Earth reveals that the government in Athens is some 230 kilometres from the island.

I didn't know that at the time, but I definitely couldn't see the coast of Greece from where I stood.

So how does a strategically significant and desirable piece of island real estate ten kilometres off the coast of Turkey come to belong to the government of a foreign nation more than two hundred kilometres away (a pretty major distance in the Balkan region, as a glance at recent historical developments will show)? As with most seemingly simple questions in this part of the world, the answer is somewhat less than simple.

'Greece' is an interesting word. In fact the modern inhabitants of that nation call it Ellada, but like it to be known officially, in English, as the Hellenic Republic. People speaking a language related to modern Greek spread throughout the region in the last millennium BCE. Various kingdoms and city-states rose and fell until most were united after conquests by the armies of Rome in the 2nd century B.C.E. Latin, of course, became the official language and so continued for many centuries. After the fall of Rome in the 5th century, the power base of the Roman Empire shifted to the eastern capital of Constantinople, and the Greek language bubbled back to prominence again, in much the same way that English did in the centuries after the Norman (French) Conquest.

The island of Lesbos continued as part of the Roman (Byzantine) empire until, with the decline of Byzantine power, it passed into the hands of, first, the Latin crusaders, and then to the Genoese in the 14th century. The Ottomans incorporated it into their empire in 1462, where it remained for some 450 years until the break-up of that empire in the early twentieth century. One important feature of Ottoman rule (in all parts of their empire) was the tolerance they granted to conquered peoples to continue using their own language and practising their own religion. They did, however, import and settle Muslim families from their Anatolian heartland to live alongside the locals.

It is with the dawning of the twentieth century and the dissolution of the Ottoman Empire that the matter seems to become more clouded. The English version of *Wikipedia*, on the subject of Lesbos, contains this laconic sentence: *'The island was conquered by the Ottoman Turks in 1462. It remained under Turkish rule until 1912 when it was ceded to Greece.'* The entry in Turkish is a little more explanatory: *During the Balkan Wars, in January 1913, Greeks occupied the island without firing a shot. It was then given to Greece under the terms of the Treaty of London, 30 May 1913. In 1922, during the exchange of populations after the Turkish War of Liberation, the Turkish population was sent to Anatolia and replaced by Greeks from the Turkish mainland* (my translation).

So what, you may ask, has all this got to do with Cyprus? Well, the first thing I'd ask you to do is to take a look at a map of the Aegean and eastern Mediterranean. Have a close look at the Greek Islands in particular, and notice how close most of them are to the Turkish mainland. Then, leaving aside other considerations, ask yourself how many other nations would accept the continuing occupation, by a foreign power, of islands so close to their own shores. The attitude of successive US governments to the island of Cuba springs to mind as an example.

But of course, as you were no doubt quick to point out, we can't leave aside other considerations. We need to delve a little into history in order to understand where we truly are in the present. As one might expect of an island with such geo-political importance, ownership has passed through many hands. Cyprus came under the sway of the Byzantine Empire in 395 CE, before falling into the hands of the Arabs for three centuries. The Byzantines reclaimed the island in 966 CE before losing it finally to a succession of Crusading princes and Venetians starting in 1191. It was from the Venetians, then, that the Ottomans seized control in 1570, despite the report in Shakespeare's *Othello* that the invading Turkish fleet had been destroyed by a storm.

As noted above, the Ottoman Empire applied a relatively enlightened policy (in the context of history) in allowing minority groups (such as Jews and Orthodox Christians) to use their own language and practise their own religion. It has been suggested by at least one historian that things might have turned out better for the Ottomans in the long run if they had been less accommodating – but there you are.

The nineteenth century was characterised by the rise of nationalism as a political force. Encouraged by the Great Powers of Europe, with an eye to their own advantage, minorities within the Ottoman Empire began to demand independence and autonomy. After the kingdom of Greece was established in 1832, other Greek peoples within the Empire (known as 'Rum' in Turkish) began increasingly to nurture the hope of a revival of former Byzantine glories.

In 1878, following a secret agreement with the increasingly desperate Ottoman government, the British occupied the island of Cyprus. 'Why?' you may ask. In fact, by the 19th century, the Mediterranean had ceased to be an Ottoman lake and had pretty much become a British one. In 1814, the island of Malta had become part of the British Empire. The territory of Gibraltar, on the south coast of Spain, has been a British possession and site of a naval base since 1713. After the opening of the Suez Canal, in 1869, and the increasing threat of Russia to British interests in India and the Near (Middle) East, Cyprus was seen as having major strategic importance. In fact, despite granting independence to the island in 1959, Britain maintains, to the present day, two military bases there at Akrotiri and Dhekelia.

In the last years of British administration after 1955, as Greek nationalists (EOKA) began a campaign of guerrilla tactics, Turkish Cypriots were used in a policing capacity by the British, and internecine violence began to escalate. Anti-Greek riots broke out in Istanbul resulting in the last major exodus of Greeks from the city.

After independence was achieved in 1960, a constitution was established creating a Greek-Turkish state in Cyprus, but violence continued, fuelled by a desire among members of the Greek community for *Enosis* (union with mainland Greece) and the perception, among the Turkish minority, that they were being driven out.

The issue came to a head on 15 July 1974 when the ruling military junta in Greece authorised a coup in Cyprus to take over the elected government and make *Enosis* a fact. There is some divergence of opinion about what happened next. The Greek position is that Turkey used this as a pretext for their military invasion; the Turks claim that they asked Britain and France to intervene to stop the violence on the island, but, receiving no reply, took the matter into their own hands. These differing claims are reflected in the words used to describe the events of July 1974, which most of the world calls 'The Turkish Invasion' but Turks refer to as 'The Peace Operation'.

4

Actions and Reactions - The Emergence of Modern Turkey

20 August 2009

A question on British history for those with an interest in the subject: What international event brought about the collapse of the victorious Liberal/Conservative coalition government after the First World War, the political demise of its heroic leader, David Lloyd George, and exile to the political wilderness of that other great hero of British politics, Winston Churchill? Not to mention the emergence of Canada as an independent nation within the British Empire?

The Chanak Incident, I hear someone cry – and they would be absolutely right! But for those of you with a more superficial interest in British history and politics, or a less persistent determination to learn about an event which receives scant attention in general histories or in biographies – let me give you a quick run-down . . .

These two English gentlemen, Churchill and Lloyd George (well, Lloyd George, it seems, was Welsh, with quite an enthusiasm for Welsh nationalism, at least when he first entered parliament), are not generally remembered with much fondness in Turkey. However, it is my contention that modern Turks should be more grateful, because, without them, it is possible that the modern Turkish Republic might never have come into being.

Of course, as with all historical events, specific dates are necessarily arbitrary, in the sense that every event has prior causes and subsequent repercussions. To understand what happened in September 1922, we need to flashback a little, to the declining years of the Ottoman Empire. In fact, the once great empire had been declining for a century or two – held together during the 19th century largely by the conflicting ambitions of the European Great Powers, who were unanimous on one thing at least: none of them wanted any of the others to get anything out of the Ottoman collapse.

'Sick' though it might have been, the empire still occupied a strategic location. The Russians desperately wanted to control the Bosporus Straits, which would give them easy access to the Mediterranean. The British, on the other hand, were pretty determined not to let them. At the outbreak of World War I, while they were both looking the other way, a maverick German admiral named Wilhelm Souchon sailed his two warships into the Black sea, hoisted an Ottoman flag, and proceeded to bombard several Russian ports. This rather forced the Ottoman government's hand. Suddenly, they found themselves at war, not only with the Russians, but also with the French and the British.

Now, I'm not writing a history of the First World War here – not even the Middle East theatres thereof, so bear with me if I skip few months, leaving aside all that bloody business on the Western Front, for example. The stalemate there did, however, bring Winston Churchill on the scene, with his grand 'Gallipoli' scheme to take the Ottomans out of the war and help organize Russia to attack the Germans from the other side.

Well, with hindsight, of course, we know the plan was a bit of a blunder – a lot of lives lost, a lot of discontent sown amongst hitherto loyal members of the British Empire, and a rather embarrassing withdrawal by Allied forces, whatever brave face we may try to put on it. But the point I want to make here is this – the Gallipoli Campaign (or the Çanakkale War, as the Turks call it) provided the opportunity for a young Turkish officer, Mustafa Kemal, to make a name for himself as a successful strategist and commander of men. Churchill's hare-brained scheme may not have done much for the Allied war effort, but it can be seen as an indispensable step on the rise to prominence of the eventual founder of the Turkish Republic. Good one, Winston!

Nevertheless, despite the efforts of Mustafa Kemal Pasha, the Ottoman Empire, its government and people, found themselves on the losing side at the end of that Great War. Victory gave the Allied leaders the opportunity they had long sought to carve up the empire's territories and distribute them among themselves. This carve-up, long planned by Britain and France, was given full expression in the Treaty of Sevres (10 August, 1920). The plan was to retain the Imperial government in Istanbul/Constantinople (to the chagrin, it may be added, of the Greeks, who refused to ratify the treaty) while giving control over the Imperial finances to the conquering Allies. Ottoman armed forces would be effectively emasculated and 'war criminals' would be brought to trial. Even the Anatolian heartland of Turkey would be divided up, with the southern coast and hinterland coming under Italian control, the south-east bordering Syria being ceded to France, and a referendum held to decide the fate of 'Kurdistan'.

So dispirited was the Ottoman government, and its people so exhausted by years of continuous war that it is possible these provisions, humiliating as they were, might have been put into effect. However, there was one last item . . . the city of Izmir and its surrounding region, and the region of Thrace, north of the Sea of Marmara to within a stone's throw of Istanbul, would be ceded to Greece – and to ensure this happened, the Greek army, encouraged and supplied by the Allies, occupied Izmir and began advancing into Anatolia.

Leaving the Greek army in Anatolia for a moment, I'd like to return to Mr Lloyd George. Our Dave apparently belonged to the Philhellene school of thought, a position popularized by the poet Lord Byron, and generally subscribed to by aristocrats who had had a love of all things classical beaten into them from an early age by the English public school system. During the 19th century, English philhellenes supported the cause of Greek independence from the Ottoman Empire, and even encouraged them in their megali idea-listic dream of recreating a Hellenic empire around the Aegean Sea.

Secure in the belief (misguided, as it turned out) that the might of the British and French was behind them, the Greeks plunged into Anatolia, intent on resurrecting their former Byzantine glory. Had they not been blinded by these visions of grandeur, it might have occurred to them that the aforementioned philhellenist gentlemen had their illusions based on a more classical, pagan, Athens-centred, ancient kind of Greekness. They would probably have had trouble getting their Church of England heads around the Byzantine Orthodox Christian variety centred on Constantinople. Anyway, it's a safe bet that the Allied powers had no intention of letting the modern Greeks get their hands on the city of Byzantine dreams. We may imagine that they were more interested in putting an end, once and for all to Turkish power, and setting up a suitably grateful puppet state in the eastern Mediterranean.

Whatever the true case may be, it's another reasonably safe bet that the event which finally fanned the spark of Turkish nationalism into flaming life, galvanised Mustafa Kemal Pasha into revolutionary action, and assisted his cause in raising an army, was this incursion into the ancestral Turkish Anatolian heartland by Greek invaders who had been finally defeated and sent packing four and a half centuries earlier.

It took a few years to get them out, of course. Mustafa Kemal freed himself from Allied-occupied Istanbul, and the puppet government of the last Ottoman Emperor, in May 1919. During the next three years, he organised a resistance movement, established an alternative nationalist Turkish government, built an army, negotiated with foreign powers (notably the new Bolshevik Russia) to supply munitions, and fought a successful war of liberation, driving the Greek Army back to Izmir.

There is considerable debate about subsequent events in that city, but most accounts agree that, for whatever reason, Allied ships (mostly British) in Izmir harbour, refused to pick up Greek military and civilian refugees from the Turkish victory. Whatever the truth of it, the Turkish army then turned north, with the intention, no doubt, and not unreasonably, of liberating Istanbul. There was, however, a small garrison of French and British troops near Çanakkale, and the British cabinet (in particular, Messrs Churchill and Lloyd George), instructed their men to turn the Turks back – in fact, threatening them with the might of the British Empire should they not go quietly.

A tricky situation, you might say, for the fledgling Turkish nation to find itself in – but Mustafa Kemal Pasha apparently decided to call the British bluff, which at this point, turned out to be exactly that. The French Prime Minister pulled his troops out, the British parliament and public expressed outrage at the thought of entering another war so soon after the last one; and the Dominions of the British Empire (most notably Canada, but with the exception of ever-loyal New Zealand) declined to get involved.

The result was the complete withdrawal of occupying forces from Istanbul, the drawing up of a new treaty (at Lausanne, Switzerland) recognizing the emergent Republic of Turkey with rather more favourable boundaries, the political humiliation of Lloyd George and Winston Churchill, and the collapse of the wartime British coalition government (one can imagine, amidst a crescendo of recriminations!).

Win and Dave were pretty much honour-bound to resign, Lloyd George, at least, never to return in any major capacity. Churchill, however, recognising his indispensability to the British people, quickly forsook the Liberal Party he had helped to destroy, and joined up with the Conservatives – and to the devil with political convictions and party loyalty. Before long he was back in full voice, demonstrating the diversity of his talents, as Chancellor of the Exchequer, and as an advocate of the enlightened use of poison gas (some years ahead of Saddam Hussein) on rebellious Kurdish tribesmen, who were perhaps not 100 percent convinced that the British Empire had any right to be in their particular neck of the woods.

Anyway, as they say, that's another story. I do think, however, that residents of modern Turkey should cast an appreciative nod in the direction of Winston Churchill and David Lloyd George as they celebrate their Day of Victory on August 30th. The camel may not fully appreciate the nature of his predicament until the last straw is dropped on his back.

5

The Liberation of Istanbul

19 September 2009

In 2007 a Turkish graphic novel named 'Son Osmanlı' (The Last Ottoman) was turned into a film named for its hero, Yandım Ali. Released under the English title of 'Knockout Ali', the film made little impact elsewhere, despite achieving considerable popularity in its home country. Not so surprising, really. The Turkish film industry is one of the largest producers of films in Europe, but few of its oeuvres find much viewership beyond the borders of the home country.

Yandım Ali is a latter-day Robin Hood figure, roaming the streets of Istanbul/Constantinople immediately after the First World War. His city, however, is under occupation, with the Sheriff of Nottingham's men replaced by the British military. If you can find your way past the Turkish accents of local actors roped in to play the parts of British officers, you see a population chafing under the injustices and oppression of a foreign invader. Ali is the handsome tough guy whose national pride cannot tolerate the bullying arrogance of the occupying forces, but his puny opposition is doomed to failure without a good King Richard to give it focus. The Lionheart's role is filled by a young Turkish officer, Mustafa Kemal, about to embark on a momentous quest to liberate his people.

Well, you're saying, I can see why that didn't attract much interest outside Turkey (except maybe among ex-pat Turkish communities in

Germany and elsewhere). It's pretty clearly a hopelessly slanted, highly romanticised piece of anti-British propaganda. And of course, romanticised and slanted it is indeed. But sometimes it is good for us to see another slant on events we think we understand, in order to appreciate the slant that has influenced our own perspective. 'O, wad some power,' said Rabbie Burns, 'the giftie gie us/ To see ourselves as others see us.' Such insight is not always a comfortable thing, but 'Yandım Ali' begs a question or two that I'd like to investigate. Once again, a trip back in time is necessary . . .

The Istanbul of Yandım Ali was, of course, the capital city of the Ottomans, the ruling elite of an empire that had exerted a major influence on the domestic and foreign policies of European nations for more than six hundred years. The empire was at its peak in the 16th and 17th centuries, only finally being turned back from the gates of Vienna in 1683. From then on its decline was gradual but inexorable, though its existence, albeit in an ailing capacity, continued to shape the policies of the Great Powers of Europe throughout the 19th century, up to and including the First World War. The workings of this influence were covered by the term, 'The Eastern Question', which can be summarised as: 'When will the Ottoman Empire finally fall apart, and which of us (i.e. the European Great Powers) is going to get what when it does?'

Two great driving forces of events in the 19th century were Nationalism and Imperialism. Clearly these forces are, in essence, mutually contradictory. As the Great Powers of Europe expanded their empires, it goes without saying that they impinged more than a little on the sovereign rights of national groups within their expanding borders. It may be said that the one thing leaders of the Great Powers agreed on was the need to suppress nationalist minorities. At the same time, however, they were not averse to employing the disruptive power of such minorities when to do so suited their own expansionist goals.

The later years of the Ottoman Empire provide several examples of this ambivalent approach to nationalist self-awareness. Contrary to the bad press they frequently receive on the subject, the Ottomans were remarkably tolerant of differences of language and religion within their borders. Of course, Islam was the official religion, and Ottoman Turkish the language of government. However, Orthodox Christians (as well as, incidentally, Armenians) and Jews were allowed to practise their religion and use their own languages and alphabets provided they paid their taxes. I would not be the first to suggest that it was this tolerance by the Ottomans of national differences within their empire that contributed to and hastened its disintegration.

However that may be, it is certainly true that the one area where the Great Powers of Europe were remarkably tolerant, even encouraging of the aspirations of nationalist minorities, was within the boundaries of the Ottoman Empire. In an earlier chapter, I touched on the support given by Britain, France and Russia to the cause of Greek independence in the 1820s. In 1827, fleets of these three nations combined to defeat the Ottoman navy, paving the way for the foundation of the modern kingdom of Greece. Why 'kingdom' you may ask? Well, because it allowed the big brother nations to install as Head of State, someone from their own ranks, the 17 year-old Bavarian Prince Otto, who became King of the new 'Greece'. Less than thirty years later, Britain and France were in league with those same Ottomans, smashing the Russians in Crimea. What had changed? Pass on another sixty years and you'll find Britain and France, back together with Russia again, intent on finishing off the Ottomans who were now supported by Germany! Make sense?

Let me give you a quick run-down. First, the Greeks. Well, they were Christians, weren't they? Obviously being oppressed by those terrible Muslim Turks. Never mind that Greek Christians within the Ottoman Empire were allowed to speak their language, practise their religion, hold important positions and get rich. But, and it's a big 'but', at least as far as Western Europeans were concerned, Greek Christianity was not the right sort. There was always a major danger that they would unite with (or be subjugated by) their Orthodox cousins, the Russians. Then there was the confusing business of what you actually mean when you say 'Greek'. Philhellenes on the continent (see the previous chapter) had a hazy idea of Greek-ness as being an ancient, classical, pagan but nonetheless romantic birthplace of modern civilisation centred on Athens. Modern Greek nationalists, on the other hand, were more inclined to imagine a medieval Orthodox Christian empire centred on Constantinople.

So, if you were a British political leader in the 19th century, you might find it convenient to give moral, and even logistical support to the cause of Greek independence, since it would be useful to have a grateful puppet-state in the eastern Mediterranean. On the other hand, you might also feel a little nervous of the southward-expanding Russians, who were encouraging, for their own ends, the nationalist aspirations of Christian minorities within the Ottoman borders. Especially since the Russian brand of Christianity had a lot more in common with those 'oppressed' brothers (and sisters).

Another complicating factor was the appearance on the stage of Europe, in the 1870s, of two 'new' powers with imperialist aspirations: Italy and Germany. Illustrating perfectly the dichotomy that existed in Europeans' minds of the time with respect to imperialism and nationalism, these two emergent powers owed their existence to the nationalist dream of uniting people with a common linguistic, racial and cultural heritage. Having achieved this goal, however, they immediately entered into competition with the older powers in the field of empire building (and, hence, of course, in overriding the nationalist ambitions of others).

It is also obvious that, as the nineteenth century gave way to the twentieth, the importance of oil as a new source of energy, added to the strategic importance of the Suez Canal for access to India, the 'jewel' in the British Imperial crown, increased the tensions and power games in the Near (Middle) East. Western Europeans are not generally known for their love of Arabs, yet they were only too ready to lionise TE Lawrence as he championed Arab nationalism against the evil Ottomans.

Well, sorry for the digression – it's not my aim to make a detailed examination of nineteenth century power politics. Just to give enough background for you to follow what I want to say about the aftermath of World War I, as it affected the country we now know as Turkey.

The European summer of 1914 was ignited by the assassination of an Austrian archduke (whatever an arch-duke may be) with little other claim to fame. By the beginning of August, all the major powers of Europe were at each other's throats, with the exception of the Ottomans who were understandably uncertain who, if anyone, they should support.

This situation was resolved for them in October largely owing, once again, to our old friend, Winston Churchill. The Ottoman navy had been a major client of British shipyards for some years, and had recently ordered two modern battleships, paid for by public subscription. Winston's brainwave was, apparently, to ensure Ottoman neutrality by 'requisitioning' these battleships for the duration of the war, and paying a kind of rent for their use in the British navy. Germany seized the opportunity to present the Ottomans with two modern warships of their own, and immediately proceeded, after hoisting the Ottoman flag, to sail across the Black Sea and bombard one or two Russian ports and bases. Not much room left for diplomatic manoeuvring after that!

Well, it took four years, and a lot of death and destruction, but the upstart Germans were eventually brought to their knees, especially after the entry of the USA into the war in 1917 (once again, if you can believe the rumours, with some fairly cold-blooded manipulation on the part of W.L.S. Churchill). Once it became obvious that they had backed the wrong horse, the Ottomans requested an armistice, which took place on October 30, 1918 on the Aegean Island of Lemnos. Perhaps they expected reasonable treatment from their former allies, especially since they hadn't actually invaded anyone else's territory – but they were to be disappointed. Within two weeks, British and French troops had occupied the Ottoman capital of Istanbul, and there they remained as an army of occupation for the next five years.

The two members of the Entente Cordiale then set about implementing plans long-held, to divide up the Ottoman Empire and erase it from the world map. The instrument used was the Treaty of Sevres, signed on 10 August 1920. Interestingly, neither the United States nor Russia was party to this treaty. Under its terms, the Ottoman government would continue to rule in name, but in reality as a political and financial puppet of the Allies (France and Britain). Ottoman 'war criminals' would be handed over to the Allies for trial and punishment. Most of the Near/Middle East, Palestine (there was no Israel in those days), Lebanon, Syria and Iraq were given as 'mandates' to Britain and France – and a mini-kingdom was established around the holy cities of Mecca and Medina, one assumes, as a sop to Arab nationalism. France also laid claim to a large chunk of modern Turkey north of Syria, while the Italians were given most of Mediterranean Anatolia, including offshore islands. A new nation-state of Armenia was to be established, with its border extending to the Black Sea around the modern Turkish port of Trabzon.

There were a few bitter pills to swallow there, you'd have to think – but representatives of the Ottoman Government duly signed. Perhaps they truly believed there was no alternative. Enter 'Yandım Ali' and

Mustafa the Lionheart! What precisely was the spark that ignited the tinder of Turkish nationalism is open to debate, but it's hard to imagine your average Mehmet on the Karaköy omnibus being pleased to see his 'Greek' neighbours and fellow citizens dancing in the streets of Istanbul (Constantinople) and Izmir (Smyrna) as they welcomed the invading forces. It is said that the French general entered Istanbul mounted on a white horse, as his conquering Turkish predecessor, had done in 1453. Perhaps the last straw was the sight of an army from mainland Greece (backed by their big brothers, Britain and France) landing on the Turkish mainland from whence their ancestors had been expelled 466 years previously.

Whatever the final cause, certain it is that Turkish nationalism was stirred into life. A four-year struggle ensued, at the end of which the Greek invaders were again expelled, and the Italian, British and French governments decided to cut their losses and withdraw. The Treaty of Sevres lapsed for want of support and was replaced by a new Treaty, signed at Lausanne, Switzerland, recognising the existence of the new Republic of Turkey. On 6 October every year, thousands of Istanbul school children have a holiday to celebrate getting their city back.

6

Benevolent Dictator?
Thinking About MK
Atatürk

19 October 2009

A t 9.05 am on 10 November life in Turkey comes to a halt. In every city, town and village throughout the country, sirens sound, traffic stops, work-places and schools fall silent, and for one minute, most of the seventy million population stand in mute respect for a president who died at that precise minute on that day in 1938.

Now I want to ask you a question. Do you even know who the political leader of your country was in that year? OK, then, a follow-up: can you think of a leader in the history of your country for whom the whole nation as one would stop and pay such respect (readers in North Korea excepted)?

Perhaps the thing that most strikes first-time visitors to Turkey is the ubiquitous presence of a dead politician. All of those aforementioned cities, towns and villages have prominent statues of Mustafa Kemal Ataturk, on horseback, in top hat and tails, as a bas-relief, or a larger-than-life bust. Every school classroom, public building and office workplace has his photograph on the wall. At some stage, the cynical question pops into our minds, is the real religion of this country Islam, football or Ataturkism?

The religious aspect of the matter is accentuated by the inscription on some of the busts and statues. 'Born 1881 . . .' We Christians know all about that. We measure our calendar according to when Jesus Christ was born, and how old he is now (since, in theory at least, he was resurrected to eternal life). But most of us don't take that very seriously these days. The difference is that Turks do! That man in the tinted photographs actually does live on, in their hearts! The leader of a one-party state who held the position of president for eighteen years until he died in office; the self-appointed leader of a nationalist resistance movement, who established his own revolutionary government which then duly elected him president. We don't have many precedents for that kind of thing in Western democracies. But scratch the surface of those democracies, and what do you find?

My father never involved himself directly in politics, but he did his duty as a responsible citizen of a democracy for which he had taken up arms in the Second World War. He always turned out to vote, supported a political party, and took an interest in the affairs of the country, especially as regards economic policy. In our household we always followed the news media coverage of election night vote counting. When dinner parties were held, the conversation regularly turned to politics and world affairs. But we don't idolise our politicians in New Zealand – and we're a little suspicious of people who do.

One topic of conversation I do remember among my father's friends when they were sounding off about the ills of the nation and the unreliability of its leaders: 'What we need,' the refrain would go, 'is a benevolent dictator.' As far as I can remember, the reasons were these:

- The country is going to the dogs;
- You can't trust our political leaders – they say one thing and do another; promise the earth and do nothing;
- Democracy is all fine and dandy, but it's not a good system for making tough decisions;
- I, in fact, know what needs to be done, but I'm too busy and/or lazy to get involved in politics;

- The only way to really get things done is to have a dictatorship. However, you can't always trust dictators to do the right thing, so ... we need a <u>benevolent</u> dictator! QED.

Interestingly, the subject cropped up in a recent issue of 'Time' Magazine. A certain Joel Stein, in an essay entitled 'Dictator of My Dreams'[1], pondered the question of whether 'America might not be better off under a dictatorship.' Now perhaps Mr Stein had his tongue in his cheek. Certainly he writes with self-effacing humour. Nevertheless, you feel you may detect a certain wistful longing in his penultimate sentence: 'But in an age of overwhelming choice, some dictatorial direction would help.'

I'm sure you've heard the same idea. You'll get a few hits if you 'google' the phrase, but most of them have to do with a business model. The only thing I came up with in a national context was Fredrick II, the Great, who ruled Prussia from 1740 to 1786. Well, he may have been a fine fellow, but, Prussia? And when you think about it, there wasn't really much democracy to be found in the world in the 18th century, so dictatorship, as a political system, wasn't such an unusual thing as it had become 150 years later.

So, there isn't much competition for the title of 'Benevolent Dictator'. Neither does there seem to be much agreement on what such a figure might look like if he or she did exist. Nor, in fact, in our age of pretty universal cynicism with respect to the trustworthiness of political leaders, is it easy to imagine even a 'benevolent' politician. We are far more inclined to be looking for ways to curb their influence than giving them the all-encompassing powers of a dictator.

Well, I'm going out on a limb, here, and I'm going to propose that Mustafa Kemal Atatürk (1881-1938), founder and first president of the Republic of Turkey, is the one leader of a significant nation in the history of the world who may actually qualify for the title. And I know I'm going to cop it from both sides here. Most Turks will reject my use of the word 'dictator'; Non-Turks will insist that a dictator is a dictator and adding the word 'benevolent' merely creates an oxymoronic nonsense. Nevertheless, I'm going to run with it.

Where to start? Probably the first thing we need to do is examine how Turks came to have this man as their political leader. And in

---

[1] 'Time', October 12, 2009

addressing this question, we need to understand that, although it may in some senses be true that the modern republic of Turkey sprang from the ashes of the former Ottoman Empire, prior to 1923 there was no political entity corresponding to modern Turkey. Just as, prior to 1870, there was no political entity corresponding to the modern state of Italy, nor a Germany prior to 1871. The difference is that Germany and Italy resulted from the amalgamation of several smaller states and kingdoms; while Turkey was the heartland and rump of a disintegrated empire.

In previous chapters I have looked at some of the processes and stages of this disintegration, so I don't intend to repeat that here. It is enough to remember that, over a period of a hundred years from approximately 1820, in spite of its leaders' best efforts to hold it together, as a result of a series of wars within and without its borders, the Ottoman Empire reached the point, with the signing of the Treaty of Sevres in 1920, where it virtually signed its own death warrant.

There was no military coup where the rightful sultan of the empire was deposed and replaced by a victorious general. Nor, however, was there an election where a sovereign nation state chose a new leader to replace the old. In fact, under the aforementioned treaty, the Ottoman Sultan would have continued to head a nominal Ottoman Empire, since clearly this suited the aspirations of the main sponsors of the treaty, Britain and France. However, it would have been a seriously shrunken, emasculated empire, whose head-of-state would have remained merely as a puppet of the victorious Western powers.

When Mustafa Kemal left the occupied capital of the Ottoman state on 19 May 1919, with an authorisation from Vahdettin, Sultan Mehmet VI, as 'Inspector of the 9th Army', his official role was ambiguous, but no doubt, in his own mind, he knew what he had to do. And, according to his recent biographer, Andrew Mango[2], he knew that he was the man to do it.

For a start, the Ottomans, in spite of past military glories, had had a hard time of it during those previous hundred years. Victories had been few and far between, and a victorious commander was something to be welcomed and cherished. Mustafa Kemal, as the successful defender of the Allies' attempted Gallipoli invasion, was one such. We can say that he had the military credentials to be taken seriously. Nevertheless, it

---

[2] 'Ataturk' The Biography of the Founder of Modern Turkey, Andrew Mango (2000)

can't have been easy to persuade his exhausted countrymen to gird up their loins for another struggle. There were others who believed in the need to fight – but few with the necessary vision and unshakeable self-confidence to inspire and unite the nationalist revival.

It is inevitable that legends will form around a successful national leader, and many are the tales told about Mustafa Kemal Atatürk: from the watch in his breast pocket that miraculously warded off a shrapnel fragment at Gallipoli; the clock in his room in Dolmabahçe Palace 'stopped' at the moment of his death; to the mystical significance of the numbers 9 and 19 in his life. It is futile but nevertheless interesting to speculate about whether such leaders are born or made. Hagiographic biographies imply that Mustafa Kemal was born to save his nation, which may, or may not be true. But undoubtedly, by the time the Greek army set foot in Izmir on 15 May 1919, he was pretty well convinced that his moment in history had arrived.

Revolutionary resistance grew around the charismatic leader and a Representative Committee was established in the central Anatolian town of Erzurum. By the time it was moved to Ankara in January 1920, Mustafa Kemal was its clear leader. By March of that year, he was in a strong enough position to declare that the Sultan's regime in Istanbul no longer represented the Turkish people, and the Revolutionary Committee was the only legal government. At the same time, he was smart enough to let other nations in the Islamic world understand that he was fighting for the Sultan (also the Muslim Caliph) who was being used as a puppet by the Allied forces. In the mean time he was negotiating with the newly formed Soviet Union for the supply of arms and munitions for the nationalist army.

It is not my purpose here to give a detailed description, nor even attempt to summarise the events of the Turkish War of Independence, which lasted from May 1919 to September 1922. It is sufficient for our purposes to note that the Greek Army was finally driven out of Anatolia. French and Italian forces also withdrew from the Marmara region as Mustafa Kemal led his troops north, leaving the British alone to prevent the liberation of Istanbul. The Turks rejected a British ultimatum to withdraw or face the consequences, and in the end, the British also chose to withdraw. As Mustafa Kemal is reputed to have predicted,

'As they had come, so did they go.' That is, pretty quietly and without a great deal of fuss.

Mustafa Kemal had been elected leader of the national struggle at Erzurum in July 1919 and president of the Grand National Assembly (we might call it the provisional republican government) in April 1920. In this capacity he swore allegiance to the Sultan and the Prophet – but there can be little doubt that his intention was to establish a republic and to institute reforms aimed at creating a secular state. And it seems equally clear that he recognised that in the short term, popular votes and democratic methods would not achieve these goals. During the course of the war with Greece, dissident elements on the Turkish side were silenced one way or another – unruly local commanders and over-zealous communist sympathisers among them. Now that victory had been won, and Mustafa Kemal was once again the hero, he was in a po-sition to carry out his goals as architect of the rebuilding of his country.

But to return to this matter of the benevolent dictator. Clearly, as well as being highly controversial, it is a self-evident oxymoron. In the normal run of things, a dictator seizes power by military means, and re-tains it by some form of terror. And, as has been discussed above, while history abounds with dictators, no one has really made a strong case for any of them having benevolence as a salient characteristic. Now un-doubtedly, Atatürk was a military man, who achieved much of his early fame through feats of arms. What sets him apart in this area is that his martial efforts were against the forces of alien powers invading his homeland. His own people gave him their whole-hearted support for this very reason – and, for the most part, appear to have given it willingly.

Furthermore, when his army had driven out the last of the invaders late in 1922, and he might have been justifiably intoxicated with success, he ignored more bellicose voices within his own new nation, and resisted the temptation to press on and try to reclaim former lost territories, con-tenting himself with defence of the Turkish heartland.

Be that as it may, it is also clear that the leader of the new Turkish Republic had powers which leaders modern democratic states can only dream of. For one thing, despite the occasional token election, he ruled as head of a one-party state to the end of his life. Opposition parties were briefly allowed (and hastily dissolved) in 1924, 1930 and again in 1934, but the first two-party election was not held until eight years after his death. Here, then, we can find the source of the decisive government for which our *'Time'* journalist, Joel Stein, has been longing.

Sovereignty is a key concept in the Turkish republic, and it is clear that their first leader believed in it on three levels: for the Turkish nation, it was his unwavering goal. Turkey had narrowly escaped subjugation by the European imperial powers, largely thanks to his efforts. In terms of his leadership, it is equally clear that he saw himself as the saviour of his nation, justified in wielding sovereign power in order to realise his vision. And on a personal level, it is of undoubted significance that he insisted on retaining sovereignty over his private life. His one attempt at marriage lasted two years and ended in divorce. He might have used his virtually absolute power to establish a dynasty but he did not. He enjoyed the comforts of modern civilisation, but accepted financial accountability, and refrained from living in oriental opulence.

During the years following his victory in the War of Liberation, Atatürk[3] transformed his new nation:

- In 1924, the Islamic Caliphate was abolished, and all members of the Ottoman dynasty were sent into exile. A national system of education was instituted marginalizing traditional Islamic schools. Religious courts were closed down, and the ban on alcohol was lifted;

- Economic development of the impoverished nation was begun on a system of state monopoly;

- In 1925, western-style clothing was required by law, with the passing of the famous 'hat law'. Dervish lodges were closed down as hotbeds of religious reaction; and the wearing of veils and headscarves by women was discouraged; the status of women was further enhanced by legislation the following year;

- A new penal code based on the Italian system was adopted, and in 1928, Islam ceased to be the official state religion. The Arabic alphabet used for Ottoman Turkish was replaced by a new Latin-based script; and the following year a committee was formed to

---

[3] Atatürk – Mustafa Kemal assumed this name after passing a law making surnames compulsory in 1934.

begin purifying the Turkish language by eradicating and replacing words of Persian and Arabic origin;

- German Jewish academics, displaced by the Nazis in the early 1930s, were welcomed into Turkey, and encouraged to assist in the westernisation of Turkish universities;

- The use of Arabic in mosques was discouraged, and the call to prayer was required to be made in Turkish after 1933;

- In 1934, Turks were required to adopt surnames, and traditional titles and ranks were abolished; the wearing of clerical dress outside of mosques and religious ceremonies was banned, and Sunday was made the day of rest in place of the traditional Muslim Friday.

There can be little doubt that this revolution in the way of life of the people could not have been achieved by a government bound by the need to cajole and appease voters. Turkey under Atatürk was a one-party state, and Atatürk was repeatedly re-elected to the role of president. Not a few dissenters and plotters against the president paid the ultimate penalty for their opposition and disloyalty. However, in Turkey, it was not the party that wielded the power, as in Soviet Russia, but the state. There was no uniformed para-military force suppressing opposition or terrorising the population. Mango says that, in his later years, '[Atatürk] behaved not like a modern dictator, but like a latter-day king, who had delegated government to his chief minister.'

When Atatürk died, on 10 November 1938, his protégé, İsmet İnönü was unanimously elected to succeed him as president of the republic. There was a huge outpouring of national grief, and seventeen nations attended his state funeral, among them, those who had been most embarrassed by his success in founding the Turkish republic. We can be sure that the cultural revolution implemented by Atatürk had its opponents. The religious establishment was a big loser, and an older generation educated in the Ottoman language must have been shocked to see linguistic and literary links to the past severed so abruptly. Yet in spite of that, the ideals of Atatürk's revolution live on in modern Turkey, and the country is a lone star of westward-leaning democratic secularism amongst its Islamic neighbour and brother states. Turks themselves, regardless of their political leanings, are in no doubt that, had it not been for Mustafa Kemal Atatürk, their country would have virtually ceased to exist. Mango prefers the term 'enlightened authoritarianism' to describe Atatürk's government – and Joel Stein would probably be equally happy with that. Whatever term is used, it is not easy to find an equivalent figure in the political history of any other nation. That is the reason for those pictures and statues adorning classroom walls and village squares all over Turkey – and the reason the country halts its normal frenzied activity for a brief moment every year on 10 November. Few nations can claim a leader with the stature of Atatürk. Turkey was lucky to get him.

7

Short, and Sweet! - The Symbolism of Ashure

19 November 2009

This chapter is necessarily short because it was written specifically for an essay competition sponsored by the publishers of a website called *Changing Turkey in a Changing World*[4], whose stated aim is 'Analysing Turkish politics and society within a global context.' If the Guinness people have a category for 'Absurdly short answers to impossibly complex questions', I think I deserve a mention for this piece. Five hundred words was the limit imposed for entries to the competition, and the question to be answered was: *Where do you locate Turkish society in the civilizational context? Is it Eastern? Islamic? Western? Post-western? Sui generis? Please explain why.*

I hereby present you with my 499-word attempt to define Turkish society, which, incidentally, was awarded first prize:

A Melange of Cultures

Each year Muslims prepare a delicacy known as ashure in remembrance of Noah and his people, who survived the flood of God's anger. Search

---

[4] http://changingturkey.com/category/the-big-idea-competition/

for the recipe of this ancient dessert. You will find many experts willing to share their knowledge – but little agreement, other than that it has a large variety of ingredients. For this reason, ashure has been used as a symbol of multi-culturalism. Yet, in the end, it is just a dessert – one item in the culinary wealth that is Turkish cuisine. How much more difficult to define the peoples currently in possession of this land lying at the meeting point of Asia and Europe!

Excavations at Çatal Höyük, near the Turkish city of Konya, have revealed a site dating from 7500 BCE, the oldest centre of civilisation on earth. The modern name, Konya, derives from ancient Iconium, which was a city in the time of the Hittite empire, around 1500 BCE. It was an important city in the kingdom of the Phrygians, in the 8th Century BCE, later falling to the Persians, and again to Alexander the Great, before being assimilated into the Roman Empire. *The Book of Acts* records that St Paul preached a sermon there around 50 CE. Its Christian history ended in the 11th century when Konya became the capital of the Seljuk Sultanate, and Muslims still visit the tomb of the Sufi mystic, Mevlana, in this iconic Turkish city.

Plunge a spade into the ground anywhere in Turkey, and you will find traces of similar antiquity. Preparations for Istanbul's year as *'European City of Culture, 2010'* were slowed by the city's archaeological riches. Work on the Metro line unearthed thousand year-old harbours and ships from Istanbul's days as capital of the Byzantine Empire. In the last thirty years, its population has swelled from three million to more than fifteen million. Shopping centres comparable to any in Europe exist in proximity to shantytowns of migrants from the Anatolian heartland, where methods of agriculture have changed little in two millennia.

The European stereotype of a Turk is the image evoked by names such as Genghis Khan – squat, swarthy, muscular Mongolian horsemen, thundering in hordes out of the Asian steppe, raping, pillaging and burning – locating themselves on the lower rungs of a rational person's ladder of civilisation. Yet even the physical characteristics of a Turk are hard to classify. Almost every shade and combination of skin, eye and hair colour will be met, and a striking range of body shapes and sizes, from Naim Süleymanoglu, the pocket Hercules weightlifter who measured 1.47 metres and won three Olympic gold medals from 1988 to

1996, to Sultan Kösem, who, at 2.47 meters, was recently recognised by the Guinness people as the world's tallest living man.

One thing can be said with certainty: attempting to glibly define Turkey and its people, and to locate them on some arbitrary continuum of civilisation is risky. Your stereotypes may bounce back to confound you.

8

A Christmas Message - Origins of Christianity

17 December 2009

A few years ago I was travelling through central and eastern Anatolia on a personal expedition to see some of the less accessible sights of Turkey: the Tomb of the Sufi mystic, Mevlana, in Konya; statues of ancients gods on the summit of Mt Nemrut; the sun setting on the waters of Lake Van; the snow-capped peak of Mt Ararat . . . and I spent a couple of days in the eastern city of Malatya. There weren't many tourists around at the time, and I don't look much like a Turk, so I attracted a certain amount of interest among the locals – especially when they found I could speak a little Turkish.

I was wandering around the bazaar, and one of the stallholders invited me to drink tea. I accepted, and soon a small crowd gathered, one of whom, it turned out, was a Hadji, a much-respected older gentleman who had made the pilgrimage to Mecca, and was clearly something of a theological authority in the neighbourhood. It was also soon clear that here was a rare opportunity to corner a Christian and interrogate him about the peculiarities of his religion. Muslims in Turkey are quite accepting of Christians and Jews, since we are all members of the same monotheistic family. Nevertheless, there are some perplexing issues.

'What's this business about Jesus being the son of God?' 'Can you just briefly explain that Holy Trinity thing?' Well, I know my Turkish wasn't so good at the time, so maybe I didn't do total justice to my western Christian heritage. I certainly felt it was a little unfair that I should be chosen as the spokesman and apologist for my religion and culture in that small group of hospitable but genuinely curious Turkish Muslims.

I was brought up in a good Christian family. I was sent off to Sunday school by church-going parents who contributed generously to the weekly collection, and even served on committees. I did my best to make sense of the stuff they used to tell us in Sunday School and Bible Class, until the age of about twelve or thirteen, when the questions seemed to demand more than the old superficial answers. I'd find myself mouthing the words of one of those creeds (Apostles' or Nicene) and wondering if I was the only one harbouring secret doubts about all those affirmations that, one assumed one was expected to believe if one was to call oneself a Christian:

I believe in God, the Father almighty,
creator of heaven and earth.
I believe in Jesus Christ, his only Son, our Lord,
who was conceived by the Holy Spirit,
born of the Virgin Mary,
suffered under Pontius Pilate,
was crucified, died, and was buried;
he descended into hell.
On the third day he rose again;
he ascended into heaven,
he is seated at the right hand of the Father,
and he will come to judge the living and the dead.
I believe in the Holy Spirit,
the holy catholic Church,
the communion of saints,
the forgiveness of sins,
the resurrection of the body,
and the life everlasting.
Amen.

Well, it's a big ask, isn't it! There's some fairly demanding stuff in there, wouldn't you say? 'Son of God', 'Born of the Virgin Mary', 'resurrection of the body' . . . It's a challenge worthy of Alice in Wonderland's Queen of Hearts, who trained herself to believe as many as six impossible things before breakfast. Not easy without that kind of determination. In fact, only two of the four Gospel authors, Matthew and Luke, make that claim about the Holy Spirit's paternity – and you can't help feeling, as you read their words, that they have the ring of something written after the fact; which, of course, they were . . . at least 60 to 80 years after.

And what about Jesus himself? Did he believe his mother was a virgin? References to 'my Father' don't count for much, because God was pretty much everybody's father figure in those days. Jesus was more inclined to talk about the 'son of man', which is a rather more modest claim, and probably has pretty much the same meaning as 'human being'.

So where do these so-called 'creeds' come from? Who concocted them? And who decided that accepting them holus bolus was the *sine qua non* of being a Christian? I remember one church minister, more adventurous and intellectually credible than most, making some attempt, from the pulpit, to reassure inquiring minds in his congregation that the words of the creed, seen in the correct light, were not as outrageous as they might at first appear. But in the end, the words are there, aren't they? You can't really weasel your way around 'descended into hell' and 'on the third day he rose again', can you? And, of course, that's exactly what the writers intended! But who were those writers?

I guess I had put all such questions on to the mental back burner long before I came to Turkey. I came here to work, unlike some who come on a search for spiritual truth: the touchingly naïve Americans who, from time to time, embark on expeditions to Mt Ararat hoping to excavate the remains of Noah's Ark; or others convinced that they are praying in the house once inhabited by the Virgin Mary. However, the very existence of such places brought those questions back to mind . . . and, surprisingly, provided unexpected answers to fundamental questions about Christianity, in a country whose population is reportedly 99% Muslim.

One thing you can't escape from in Turkey is the reality of the early Christian church, and all those places and people: Peter, Paul, John, Mary, Ephesus, Antioch, Galatia . . . At the same time, you come to see also how much the development of Christianity was tied up with its acceptance as a state religion by the Roman Empire centred on Constantinople, and the political realities of that time and place. So, it's an interesting paradox. On the one hand, you are confronted with the undeniable reality of people, places and events that gave birth to the Christian religion. On the other, you also see that much of the dogma of that religion, the articles of faith which one was expected to espouse as a true believer, were formulated and codified long after the founding events by committees of priests and politicians, for what might often have been pragmatic rather than spiritual reasons.

So let's start with the real places and people. The Tigris and Euphrates are branches of the river that, according to *Genesis*, flowed out of the Garden of Eden – and both rise in eastern Anatolia. You'll be unlikely to find remains of Noah's Ark, but Mt Ararat can definitely be seen rising to 5185 metres near the border of Turkey and Iran. Head south and west and you will come to the city of Urfa, where you will find a queue of faithful Muslims waiting to enter a cave deemed to be the birthplace of the prophet Abraham.

OK, that old stuff, you may say. But what about the New Testament, the actual Christian business? Well, keep heading west towards the Mediterranean coast and you will find yourself in Antakya, the ancient city of Antioch, the base of St Paul's missionary activities. You can visit the grotto-church of St Peter, in this city where Christians were, so the story goes, first actually called 'Christians'. Somewhat more accessible to the tourist resorts of Aegean Turkey lies the town of Selçuk, a short drive or a middling walk from the site of Ephesus, one of the best-preserved cities of the ancient world. It was also the location of one of the Seven Churches of Revelation, all of which are to be found not far away in other parts of western Turkey. There is a widely accepted tradition that the apostle John, charged by the dying Jesus with the care of his mother, Mary, took her eventually to Ephesus, where they both drew their last breaths. Certain it is that the Byzantine Emperor Justinian I had a basilica church built there in the 6th century over what was believed to be John's final resting place – not far from a restored house held by many to have been the last dwelling of Jesus's mother, Mary.

I could go on, but you get the point. It was a long time ago, but these are real people, and real places we are talking about here. However, things start getting a little murky when you move from history and geography, into the realms of faith, theology and dogma. Certainly the new religion took off, for one reason and another, and began to be seen by the Romans, who controlled most of the Mediterranean world (and much of Europe) in those days, as a threat to their established way-of-life. The story of the violinist-Emperor Nero is well known – he is said to have passed blame for his own torching of the Imperial City on to the Christian community, which then justified an orgy of bloodthirsty torture and execution lasting from 64-68 CE. More open to debate is the theory that, far from terminating the new religion, Nero's excesses of violent persecution actually aroused sympathy for the oppressed Christians, and gave the movement strength.

Persecution continued, however, until the reign of Constantine I. He it was who founded the city of Constantinople in 330 CE, and is called 'the Great' on account of being the first Christian Roman Emperor. Again, there is some debate about how he acquired his new faith, but clearly, by this point in history, being a Christian had become rather more socially acceptable. The special relationship of a man with his mother is proverbial in the Mediterranean world, and it is known that Constantine's mother was a Christian. A grander, and rather more 'imperial' tale asserts that, on the eve of battle against his rival Maxentius, to unite the Empire after a period of division, Constantine had a dream instructing him to display the symbolic letters of Christ on his soldiers' shields. His troops won the battle, and the rest, as they say, is history.

From here began the majestic pageant of Christianity leading to its eventual cultural domination of the world – or its downward slide into politics and corruption, depending on your point of view. Clearly, once Christianity had become the state religion of the Roman Empire, there was a need for an orthodox position and a clearly delineated set of beliefs. The first problem that required solving was what to do about the bishops and other high-ranking churchmen who had not only recanted their faith during the years of persecution, but, in some cases, to save their own skins, had actually dobbed in members of their own congregations. Certain purists, known as 'Donatists', were, apparently, of the opinion that such turncoats should not be allowed back into the church now that the bad times were over. As we might imagine, however, there are advantages for an emperor in having high-ranking subordinates who can be relied on to toe the party line – and not only were the former apostates allowed back, but many of them returned to high office. Needless to say, there would have been unhappiness in some quarters with this decision.

Nevertheless, having established a coterie of bishops to lead his new institutionalised state church, Constantine called them together in the city of Nicaea in 325 CE. Nicaea, incidentally, still exists as Iznik in modern Turkey, and was the location of a major ceramics industry during Ottoman times. But not to digress, the Council of Nicaea was charged with laying down a code of beliefs for the Church, and in doing so, to alienate heretics who might threaten the state monopoly. The 'heresy' of Gnosticism had already been dealt with in the previous century; Gnosticism being a mystical religious philosophy from pre-Christian times, which tended to avoid the more literal-minded excesses of mainstream Christianity. Having got rid of this threat, it was really just a matter of haggling over details, though these details did cause some serious splitting of the one 'holy catholic church'.

The Nicene gathering had to deal with the so-called 'Arian' heresy. Well, I have no intention of trying to explain this or any of the subsequent theories in a similar vein which these and later holy fathers debated at great length, and, in their infinite wisdom, handed down decisions on. Some of them concerned the perplexing doctrine of the Holy Trinity – in particular, what exactly was the nature of the three beings, Father, Son and Holy Ghost; and what were their relationships to each other, if, that is, they were actually separate at all, which they weren't, or aren't. As Spike Milligan used to say, 'It's all rather confusing, really!'

Now you might think, with me, that some matters are better left alone, as being beyond the powers of mere mortals to comprehend; and the details might safely be left to the individual understanding of willing believers. It wasn't so, however, in the institutionalising Christian Church. The all-knowing holy fathers apparently felt themselves quite capable of making pronouncements on such matters, and began the tradition of formulating creeds for the guidance of future generations. And the wording of these creeds, far from being broad enough to encompass a spectrum of individual belief, was, on the contrary, agonised over at great length, so as to specifically proscribe any deviation from the 'true path', as determined by the aforesaid holy fathers.

Well, it's a complex but interesting business. Clearly, the process I have touched on here did not end in 325 CE at Iznik. It continued at Chalcedon (modern Kadıköy) in 451 CE, and at other councils throughout the days of the Byzantine Roman Empire. The situation was further complicated by the 'Great Schism' of 1054 CE, when Western and Eastern Christendom decided to go their separate ways; and again in the aftermath of the Protestant Reformation of the 16th century – but we can leave those discussions for another day.

In summary, however, what I want to say is this: I feel a whole lot more comfortable about my Western religio-cultural heritage since coming to Turkey. I have a better understanding of the relationship between the world's three great monotheistic religions. I have visited places that have added a sense of reality and objectivity to the traditions and culture that I absorbed with the air I breathed through my childhood and education. I have come to see that much of what bothered me, as an inquiring adolescent, about the Christian Church, is, to say the least, of questionable relevance to the philosophy and message of its eponymous founder. And if anything I have said makes you feel a little better in the coming weeks of the festive season, then I will feel my time has been well spent.

9

Timeo Danaos et Dona Ferentes - It's All Greek to Me

18 January 2010

I used to think I had a handle on the Ancient Greeks and Romans. Not that I'm a great classicist, but I did spend a few years at school studying Latin, so I knew, for example:

- The Greeks organised themselves in city states, rather than an empire, as the Romans did;

- The Greeks came before the Romans (well, the Romans conquered the Greeks, which amounts to the same thing, I suppose);

- The Latin language more or less took over from the Greek (at least with regard to the classical world);

- The Roman Empire fell to the barbarians in the 5th century CE;

- Ancient Greece was an area that more or less corresponded to modern Greece.

Then I came to Turkey. The first thing I noticed was that Turks have two words in common use for 'Greek': 'Yunan' and 'Rum'. The first word denotes the people who live in the modern state of Greece: while the second refers to the Greek-speaking people who live (or rather, for the most part, lived) in Istanbul and Anatolia. If you want to talk about the ancient ones, it gets more complicated.

The second thing I noticed as I wandered around ancient structures in Istanbul was that there were, indeed, inscriptions in Latin (as you would expect in a city that was once the capital of the Roman Empire); but there were far more inscriptions in Greek, also pretty ancient, but clearly of a later date than the Latin ones.

I don't know about you, but I hate things like this. They make me want to find out why – so here's where I've got to so far …

A quick peek at *Wikipedia* will inform you that there is quite a host of names that have been applied over several millennia to the people we, in English, are happy to think of as 'Greek'. The one the (modern) Greeks themselves generally prefer is *Hellene*, which dates back to a mythological origin (somewhat similar to the role played by *Hawaiiki* in Polynesian cultures). The mythical patriarch, Hellen, apparently begat four sons, who respectively sired the eponymous tribes, *Aeolian, Dorian, Achaean* and *Ionian*. Our word 'Greek' derives from the Latin word for the Greek-speaking people who migrated to Italy in the 8th century BCE. Homer, so I'm told, used the words *Argives* and *Danaos*, to refer to the guys who came to Troy in the thousand ships launched by the face of their kidnapped princess, Helen (with one 'l'). Persians, apparently, used the word *Yunani* (from *Ionian*), and you will remember that this is one of the words modern Turks use. Ottomans, I gather, used the word 'Roman' (*Rum*) for their 'Greek' neighbours (for reasons which will be examined below), and this is the origin of the other word used in modern Turkish.

So … Luckily, we have the Julietian principle to apply here: *'a rose by any other name would smell as sweet'*. Unfortunately, it's rather easier to agree on what a rose is, than to settle on a concept of Greek-ness that everyone will accept. Still, never let it be said that this writer shied away from a tricky task.

The people that we like to refer to as 'Greek' in English can trace their roots way back to tribes that settled in the 'Greek' peninsula in prehistoric times (2000-1500 BCE) after coming from ... no one is very sure where. However, one point is important to stress from the outset: there is no easily defined continuity of geographical location and religion, even of language and culture, which can be traced from that time to this.

The culture that most English-speakers think of as 'Ancient Greek' began to appear after what is often referred to as the 'Dark Age', around 800 BCE. For various reasons, apparently involving food shortages and violence, 'Greek' speaking peoples began to move into Italy and across the Aegean to Asia Minor (now Turkey) and the region of the Black Sea. At this time, there was undoubtedly a common base of language and culture that was inevitably influenced by that of the peoples with whom they came in contact in their new lands.

Another point must be emphasised here. Despite the common language and culture, these 'Ancient Greek' peoples organised themselves in city-states, which, not infrequently, fought each other. There was no overall coming-together into anything we would recognise as a nation, let alone an empire. While there were loose confederations of city-states when the need arose to face a common enemy (such as the Persians), these federations themselves fought each other in struggles for supremacy.

I have no intention of trying to detail the to-ings and fro-ings of these city-states (Athens, Sparta, Ephesus, Miletus and so on) and leagues (Delian, Peloponnesian, Ionian etc). It is sufficient for my purpose to note that there were, in what we like to think of as 'Classical Greek' times, city-states on both sides of the Aegean Sea, and that those on the eastern coast made as great a contribution to the civilisation as did those on the so-called 'Greek mainland'.

There seems to be much debate about the setting of dates for 'classical' Greek civilisation. While some scholars claim a continuity from the Minoans (around 2700 BCE) through to the adoption of Christianity (4th century CE), others prefer to focus on important changes that create distinctly different cultural and political entities. Should we consider the currently dominant USA as part of the continuing supremacy of English culture and civilisation; or is the US a distinct entity that superseded the British Empire as the major world power? I ask merely to illustrate the nature of the problem.

Whatever your answer, it is clear that the centres of 'Greek' civilisation and culture continued to move east. Alexander the Great, who hailed from Macedonia, conquered Syria, Egypt, Mesopotamia and Persia, even venturing as far as India. It's easy to overlook the fact that the guy died when he was 32, and his so-called empire lasted 10 years at the most. Nevertheless, his conquests did usher in the Hellenistic Age, whose cultural centres were Antioch (in modern Turkey) and Alexandria (in Egypt). The language and culture of this age we tend to consider 'Greek' – but how 'Greek', in fact, were they?

Coming back to Greece itself (in the modern sense of the word), 'mainland Greece' passed from Macedonian control into the hands of the Roman Republic / Empire in 146 BCE. Undoubtedly 'Greek' civilisation was enormously influential in helping to shape the culture, religion and political institutions of the Roman Empire. Nevertheless, again, it must be noted that political control was in the hands of the Romans, and the language of power was Latin.

Well, I'm skipping a few more centuries while Rome held indubitable sway over most of the lands under consideration here. We're passing forward to 330 CE when the Roman Emperor, Constantine I built his 'New Rome' on the site of the earlier city of Byzantium, and it became Constantinople. At this point, there's no doubt that we are still talking about the Roman Empire. But, over the next few years, strange things happened. First, Constantine began to tolerate Christians; then his successor, Theodosius I, made Christianity the state religion in 380 CE. Parallel to the spread of the new religion, the city of Rome lost its political dominance and 'Greek' began to bubble back to the surface as the language of Constantinople, and hence the Roman Empire.

So, the Greeks are back, you may think – but I'm sorry, it ain't that easy. Despite the fact that they were using 'Greek' as their language, these people (I'm avoiding the use of a label here, for reasons which will become clear as we go) perversely continued to think of and call themselves Romans. Their neighbours to the east, Persians and the emerging Islamic world, also apparently continued to think of them as 'Romans'.

It was in the West, however, that serious problems of perception and nomenclature began to emerge. First we have 'The Fall of the Roman Empire', often dated at 476 CE. But clearly those Easterners continued to think of themselves as the Roman Empire until their pretensions were finally put to rest by the Ottoman Turks in 1453. Then we have the 'Christianisation' of the Roman Empire, which was a good thing, of course, since it put an end to all that persecution and feeding to the lions and what not (which was clearly a bad thing). But on the other hand, it also put an end to the glorious 'classical' civilisation of Greece and Rome (pagan and polytheistic, of course), which assumed greater and greater significance and influence in Europe after the Renaissance - so perhaps 'Christianisation' wasn't such a good thing. And then there was the emerging rivalry between the Church of Rome and their Eastern cousins in Constantinople, which resulted in the 'Great Schism' in 1054. From this point it was clearly impossible for Westerners to think of those guys as 'Roman'. Not only was the Western Church 'Roman', but a kind of virtual 'Holy Roman Empire' had begun to emerge in the 9th century, which didn't want any other claimants to the title (never mind that the claim may have had a better foundation). The best way to undermine their claim was to highlight the errant nature of their brand of Christianity, and the fact that their language was Greek, not Latin. So, Europeans at this time tended to refer to them disparagingly as 'Greeks'.

This usage continued pretty much into the 19th century, despite the fact that some scholars had begun to employ the word 'Byzantine' for the Greek-speaking, Eastern Orthodox empire centred on Constantinople. So where did that word come from? Well, we know that it was the name of the 'Greek' city whose site was taken over when Constantine wanted a location for his 'New Rome' in the east. But that was 330 CE – why bring back a name that had long since fallen out of use? It's a bit like calling Paris, 'Lutetia', apparently the name it went under in Roman times. I love Lutetia in the springtime. Huh?

See, the thing is you've been calling this Roman Empire, 'Greek' for centuries, which was no big problem so long as the only other 'Greek' thing you had to worry about was a classical civilisation that had existed a couple of millennia earlier. But suddenly, in the 1820s, you get the opportunity to assist the disintegration of a contemporary empire whose continued existence is getting in the way of your own imperialist expansion, namely, the Ottoman Empire. Unfortunately, your big opportunity involves helping to establish a new state on the Mediterranean peninsula you like to think of as the home of 'Greek' civilisation, and what can you call this new kingdom if not 'Greece' - especially since, by doing so you will guarantee the support of your own educated elite who have a well-entrenched love of everything (Ancient) 'Greek'. Incidentally, as noted above, the modern 'Greeks' don't use a word in any way resembling 'Greece' when speaking of their own country. But in English, at least, you've now got three 'Greeks': ancient, medieval and modern! None of them having much more in common with each other than do the ancient Germanic tribes, Anglo-Saxons and the modern United Kingdom.

Obviously, the best solution was to rename the most inconvenient of the three: hence the reappearance of the word 'Byzantine' to refer to the eastern Roman Empire that had continued to exist for a thousand years after the fall of the Western one. Hey presto! Talk about rewriting history!

Well, after reading that meandering and staggeringly outrageous summary of five thousand years of history, you may be forgiven for asking, what's your point, mate? For that I'd like to return to the words of my title for this piece: *'Timeo Danaos et dona ferentes' (I'm wary of Danaos, even when they bring gifts)*. The words were reportedly spoken by the Trojan priest Laocoön warning his people of the dangers of the Trojan (or more correctly, 'Greek') horse. They didn't listen, of course – and the main reason was because shortly after uttering his warning, Laocoön and his two sons were strangled by monstrous sea serpents, a misfortune interpreted by contemporaries as a sign of divine disapproval. Well, gods move in mysterious ways, as we know – but the fact remains that old Laocoön's advice turned out to have been pretty sound. You may know the statue, which is quite famous. Laocoön used the word 'Danaos', usually translated into English as 'Greeks' – and we may take the fate of him and his sons as a warning to exercise caution when we ourselves use the word 'Greek'.

10

Religion in Turkey

21 February 2010

The Turkish government has recently announced an official opening of discussions on the subject of Alevism, the second-largest religious group in the country after the majority Sunni Muslims. This 'açılım' in Turkish, represents a significant step forward for Alevis, who have experienced repression and even persecution, not only in the Republican period, but earlier, under the Ottoman regime.

I'm happy about this new spirit of openness that seems to be pervading Turkey's political scene these days. There may be bumps in the road to begin with, but in the end, good will come of it. I've been doing a little research into the Alevi sect, and various sources confirmed what I had previously heard: that there are ten to twenty million of these people living in the Republic. Well, even if you take the lower figure, that's a significant group in a population of around seventy million.

Still, you'd have to wonder why the figures couldn't be a little more precise, especially in a country that takes regular censuses, and likes to see a citizen's religious affiliation on all forms of personal ID. I was also intrigued to note that the origins of the Alevi faith are controversial, and apparently it is even hard to define precisely what they believe.

It is generally accepted that Alevism is closer to Shi'i Islam than to the Sunni variety (the majority in Turkey); and that it has close ties to the mystical Sufism of the 13th century saint, Hadji Bektash Veli. Some sources, however, suggest that it predates Islam, and has its roots in an earlier folk religion, perhaps Persian; and that it was influenced by close contact with the various strands of Christianity which were developing and separating in the early days of the Roman/Byzantine Empire.

It's not my intention here to examine, in any detail, the tenets of faith of the Alevis, even if they had been clearly codified; but some general concepts have a certain appeal:

- Love and respect for all people (the important thing, apparently, is not religion, but being a human being)

- Tolerance towards other religions and ethnic groups (If you hurt another person, the ritual prayers you have done are counted as worthless)

- Respect for working people (The greatest act of worship is to work)

- Equality of men and women, who pray side by side. Monogamy is practised.[5]

- They even, it is said, enjoy a drink now and again, and apparently consider their stricter Sunni brethren as unnecessarily rigid in their code of Islamic conduct.

Well, you may feel inclined to wonder why people holding such apparently innocuous (perhaps even laudable) beliefs would need to be suppressed or persecuted. As usual, the more you dig in this remarkable country, whether literally or metaphorically, the more details you unearth, and the more complicated the story seems to become. However, if you have read this far, you will likely have observed that my aim is to seek the overview, the big picture, rather than to lose my thread in scholarly minutiae.

So, I'm going to jump to an issue which generates a great deal of heat (even parliamentary fisticuffs) in contemporary Turkey – the question of whether the ruling AK Party has a hidden agenda aimed at dismantling the secular state and substituting Islamic Shariah law. 'What's the connection?' you may ask, and of course, I'm going to tell you. Once

---

[5] http://en.wikipedia.org/wiki/Alevi

again, I have no intention of plunging into the mire of Turkish politics, and examining the rights and wrongs of women wearing headscarves, or defending the record of a government that slew the dragon of hyperinflation, and kept Turkey out of the Iraq invasion without unduly damaging its friendship with America. Party affiliates are quite capable of dealing with these issues. Rather, I want to examine the deeper-seated reason why I believe Turkey will never descend into Islamic fundamentalism.

The reason is, in my opinion, the incredibly broad-based, eclectic nature of religion in this part of the world variously referred to as Asia Minor, Anatolia and the Republic of Turkey. The Alevi religion, so briefly outlined above, seems to me a microcosm of the processes that have shaped the beliefs of the people who now inhabit this ancient land, and resist all attempts to box and categorise them.

A short anecdote to illustrate my point, found in a popular Turkish daily newspaper:

Hadji Burhanettin lives in the east Anatolian town of Doğubeyazit. The word Hadji before his name tells us that he has made the pilgrimage to Mecca, which gives him a certain lay authority in matters of religion. His two sons came to Istanbul to start a business, and decided that manufacturing denim jeans was the way to go. Of course, it's a competitive market, and you need to position your product carefully. According to the story, the lads decided to produce the world's sexiest jeans, and named their brand 'G-Point' (I think they meant to say 'G-Spot' but both words have the same meaning in Turkish), with a stylized male arrow symbol as their logo. At first, their father was furious. How would he maintain the gravitas of his Hadji status when local friends and neighbours found out what his sons were up to in the sin capital of Turkey? Apparently, however, as money from sales of the sexy apparel began to flow, the patriarch found it in his heart to overcome his initial scruples and accept the obvious sign of divine approval.

There is an admirable pragmatism there, wouldn't you agree? Even if the logic may be a little doctrinally unorthodox. Clearly, if it wasn't ok with God, He wouldn't let the guy's sons make a profit. But I don't want to make light of religion in Turkey. Rather, I want to look briefly at the forces that have moulded it, and thereby come at an explanation of why things are as they are.

The people call their country 'Türkiye', the land of Turks – and while, prior to the First World War they were happy enough to consider themselves subjects of a diverse Ottoman Empire, they have spent the last 87 years working to persuade themselves that 'Turks' is what they are. We 'Europeans' know that 'Turks' were part of the heathen horde that swarmed out of the Central Asian steppes wreaking mayhem and terror on Christendom and Western civilization until they were finally turned back from the gates of Vienna in 1683. Well, we may have been hazy about the exact date, but you know what I mean, right?

Turks themselves seem, for the most part, relatively content these days to accept a variation of the same theme, with a few details added, and warrior heroism substituted for brutish barbarianism. Back in Central Asia, of course, the religion was shamanism, but on the way westwards they became Muslim, defeated the Roman/Byzantine Empire, set up their own Ottoman Empire and eventually mutated into the present Republic of Turkey. Of course, as gross over-simplifications go, that one is staggering in its presumptuousness. Nevertheless, while it may omit one or two details, I submit that the overall picture would not be unacceptable.

Most Turks would be surprised to learn, then, that their Turkic ancestors, in their advance along the Silk Route, became Buddhist for a time, and were undoubtedly influenced by other religions moving in the opposite direction, Zoroastrianism, Nestorian Christianity and Manichaeism to name but three, before settling on Islam after prolonged contact with Arab armies and culture moving east[6]. It has been suggested that the adoption of Buddhism first, and later Islam by Turkic leaders may be attributable more to the desire for a unifying religion to solidify their growing temporal power, than to higher spiritual motives, and they wouldn't be the only national leaders to have adopted that approach. And then there was the influence exerted on slave warriors in the service of Arab and Persian armies. At the same time, conversion to the new religion was made easier by aspects of theological concurrence with the old one, a point I want to return to later.

Anyway, from here (Bactria, Sogdia and other little remembered Central Asian states) it is a mere hop step and a jump to the eastern

---

[6] 'The Berzin Archives': http://www.berzinarchives.com/web/en/archives/study/islam/historical_interaction/overviews/buddhism_turkic.html

border of the Byzantine Empire, where the Seljuk Sultan Alp Arslan met and defeated in battle the heirs of the Roman Empire, who had ruled the eastern lands for six hundred years after the fall of Rome. The year was 1071, and it marks the beginning of the Turkish conquest of Anatolia, and the beginning of the end of the eastern Roman/Byzantine Empire.

We can say that what followed was a gradual process whereby a predominantly Muslim Turkish-speaking Anatolia replaced the earlier Christian Greek-speaking one. However, already we have mentioned some of the influences that influenced the development of the Turkish brand of Islam that entered Anatolia at this time. Also, it is likely that, not only had these Turks lost their central Asian racial purity from centuries of miscegenation by the time they invaded Anatolia, but that the process continued after their arrival, and continues to this day.

Leaving aside the mixing of races and cultures that undoubtedly followed the invasion of Anatolia, let us look briefly at some of the religious interactions that took place.

We have already mentioned Zoroastrianism in passing. This was the predominant religion of the Iranian/Persian peoples, and its origins trace back to the prophet Zoroaster (Zarathustra – *Zerdüst* in Turkish) at least a thousand years before the Christian Era. It is sometimes claimed that Zoroastrianism was the world's first monotheistic religion, and that many fundamental beliefs of Judaism, Islam and Christianity are derived from it. Unlike its successors, however, Zoroastrianism was apparently not 'monolithic' – i.e. there was some scope for divergence of opinion among believers without the need for excommunication or other forms of compulsion.

It is likely that the religion known as Gnosticism also sprang from this root. It seems to have been a more elitist set of beliefs, again, lacking a single strict dogma. While Gnosticism absorbed aspects of Christianity, it apparently placed more emphasis on the teachings of Jesus rather than his death and resurrection. Its growth as a religion kept pace with that of Christianity in the early centuries, but, lacking a central organization, it fell prey to oppression and persecution once its rival became the official state religion - a sad but typical illustration of how the oppressed are only too happy to assume the role of the oppressor as soon as the opportunity presents itself.

One thing that is very clear is that there has been, for millennia, a struggle, in this part of the world, between what one might consider the true nature of religion (the essentially personal search which attempts to give meaning to an apparently chaotic universe through an understanding of the material and spiritual natures of humanity), and the desire of succeeding rulers to impose a unified doctrine and system of religious observance which would give cohesion (not to say malleability) to their subject peoples.

One of the early great heretics of the Christian church was a gentleman by the name of Marcion, a 2nd century theologian who lived in the Black Sea city of Sinope. The essence of his teachings was that the Hebrew God of the Old Testament and the Heavenly Father of the New Testament were separate – the latter being the superior deity, while the capricious, vengeful Yahweh was a lesser force – the demiurge that created the material world. What happened to Marcion? He was excommunicated by the mainstream church, and his teachings suppressed.

Another sect of Gnosticism that acquired a following for a time was Manichaeism, inspired by its prophet Mani, who lived in the 3rd century CE. Again it was perceived as a serious threat by orthodox Christians, but perhaps contained within it the seeds of its own downfall, encouraging, as it apparently did, strict ascetic practices and even celibacy. Women, it seems 'were considered forces of darkness, binding men to the flesh'[7], which also seems unlikely to prove successful in the long-term from an evolutionary point-of-view, but may have spawned ideas that seem to persist among some Muslim believers.

In our wanderings through Central Asia earlier, we came across a sect of Christians known as Nestorians. These were followers of another reject from mainstream Christianity, Archbishop Nestor of Constantinople, who fell foul of his brethren for advancing the dangerous heresy that it might not be a hundred percent accurate to call Mary the 'Mother of God'. I have to admit I have wondered about that myself from time to time. In my travels in Turkey, I couldn't help noticing that the area of Aegean Turkey where Mary is reputed to have spent her last years was also important in the worship of Artemis and her divine predecessor, Cybele. Artemis was a complex creature, noted for her virginity as well as celebrated as a mother goddess – and known locally as

---

[7] 'Crystalinks': http://www.crystalinks.com/manichaeism.html

the Lady of Ephesus. Cybele was an earlier Phrygian earth mother deity associated with fertility, sometimes referred to as the Mother of the Mountain. Given that it is generally easier to convert people to a new religion if you can show major correspondences with their own, you could be forgiven for thinking that the process may have been at work around here. 'Hey, that's a coincidence. We've got her in our religion too – only we call her Mary!'

But to return to the Nestorians and their heretical brethren: one thing that these various sects, cults and religious deviants did achieve – it is generally accepted that the creeds formulated by Ecumenical Councils of the early institutionalised Christian church at such places as Chalcedon (Kadıköy), Ephesus and Nicaea (İznik) were a direct response to the threats they posed. So, the strange, surreal, somewhat over-the-top articles of faith that one is expected to ascribe to as a Christian reciting the Nicene or Apostles' Creed can be understood as a kind of legalese trickery to weed out heretics and deviants who might threaten the unity of the new state-sponsored religion.

Anyway, the result was a host of breakaway groups establishing their own forms of 'orthodoxy' – Syriacs, Copts, Armenians and so on – not forgetting the Roman Catholics themselves, who made their final split in 1054. But I'm getting ahead of myself here. What about the Muslims, I hear you asking. Weren't you, in fact, writing about them? And of course you are right. But it is important to recognise that these two religions, Christian and Muslim, lived side by side in Anatolia for more than eight hundred years, and for sure, their beliefs and practices rubbed off on each other. Islam, for example, is notoriously unsympathetic to anything smacking of idolatry – statues or pictures of divinities or any human beings for that matter. Undoubtedly it was a reaction to the growing popularity and power of the new religion that produced the iconoclastic movement and led to the destruction of statues, images, icons, frescos and so on in the Byzantine Christian Church in the 8th century CE.

On the other hand, Muslims in Turkey have a rather more tolerant approach to the consumption of alcohol than their co-religionists elsewhere. Religious authorities in Turkey clearly feel the need to remind visitors to certain tombs that prayers should be addressed to God rather than to a (dead) human, and that the tying of pieces of cloth to nearby trees is discouraged. Nevertheless, these and other practices persist, and suggest a survival of belief in the intercession of saints, and probably more ancient folk customs.

The 13th and 14th centuries in Anatolia are notable for the rise of a mystical offshoot of mainstream Islam, Sufism. Hadji Bektash Veli and the poet Yunus Emre, for example, proposed that a person could draw nearer to the divine during his/her mortal life by following a certain path under the guidance of a spiritual master or 'father'. Undoubtedly, the belief that enlightenment is more readily found as a result of a personal search than by following state-defined practices is strongly embedded in Turkish culture. Mustafa Kemal Atatürk, the founder of the modern Turkish Republic, banned, however, in 1925, all Sufi orders, and shut down their lodges. There is an irony here, in that followers of these orders, like the Alevis, tend to support the secular republic, on the grounds that it is more likely to extend tolerance than a monolithic Sunni establishment. Perhaps their faith and persistence are about to be rewarded.

Whatever the outcome for the Alevis themselves, I see the new spirit of openness in debate on this and other issues long swept under the carpet, as perhaps heralding a new maturity in the development of democracy in this controversial and ambiguous meeting place of Europe and Asia. It is also interesting that the opening of such issues to discussion has been instigated by a government often accused by secular Turks of supporting a conspiracy to reintroduce Shariah law. In the end, I have confidence in Turkish people themselves. Hadji Burhanettin back east in Doğubeyazit is not likely to let religious beliefs be imposed on him by outsiders who think they know better.

11

The Turkey-Israel Connection

20 March 2010

In January 2009 the Turkish Prime Minister, Recep Tayyip Erdoğan attracted considerable media attention, at home and abroad, for his spat with the Israeli Premier, Shimon Peres, at the Davos World Economic Forum. Apparently, Mr Erdoğan couldn't resist taking the opportunity to berate his Israeli counterpart for his country's recent actions in the Gaza War. Undoubtedly, there has been a cooling of relations between Turkey and Israel in recent years, especially since the accession to power of Mr Erdoğan's AK (Justice and Development) Party.

Perhaps, then, it's a good time to take a look at this event in the broader context of history, particularly at a time when Turkey is being increasingly challenged to accept the accusation of 'genocide' against the Armenian people.

One important point that must be noted at the outset, of course, is that both Turkey and Israel are relatively 'new' nations – the Republic of Turkey was founded as recently as 1923, while Israel became a nation in 1948. At the same time, however, it must also be recognised that the peoples of these two 'modern' states have lived as neighbours for more than a millennium. Turkic invaders entered Anatolia in force after defeating the armies of the Byzantine Roman Empire in 1071 CE. Already Muslim, they mixed and intermarried with the predominantly Christian peoples they had conquered, establishing states and empires culminating in the six-hundred-year Ottoman Empire, which lasted until it was finally dissolved after the end of the First World War. It is probably fitting, then, that its successor state, the Turkish Republic, was the first Muslim country to recognise officially the fledgling nation of Israel.

In the previous chapter, we looked at the complex procession and interplay of religions that have taken place in this part of the world over three millennia of history. The so-called 'clash of cultures', referring to the face-off between the Christian West and the Islamic East, is largely a western construct. Its roots lie in the desire of the medieval Bishops of Rome (Popes) to add the muscle of temporal power to their, one suspects, less satisfying spiritual leadership. In the Near and Middle East, it has been a different story.

For a start, the Muslim religion always recognised the debt it owed to its predecessor faiths, Judaism and Christianity. To Muslims, Jews and Christians are also 'people of the book' – followers of a great monotheistic belief system with shared history and common prophets. The 'Christian' crusades of the 11th to the 13th centuries, it can be argued, were more attempts to unite Western Christendom under the Popes of Rome, and assert its superiority over the East, whatever faith they espoused, than the more commonly held belief of a confederation of the righteous aiming to free the Holy Lands from heathens and unbelievers. As evidence of this, we can take the fact that the army of the Fourth Crusade took time, on its way to fight the Muslims, to besiege, conquer and despoil the Christian capital of Constantinople, 250 years before the Muslim Ottomans set foot in it. It has also been argued that, prior to the Crusades, genuine Christian pilgrims from other lands were not prevented from visiting and paying homage at sacred sites in the city that is sacred to all three religions.

Little of this, however, directly concerns modern Turkey. Of much more relevance to our discussion here are the actions of the Ottoman Empire since, at least in Western eyes, there is an undeniable connection between the two. 1453 is one of those dates in history that are interpreted by some as marking key transitions from one age to another. In this case, it was the year that the Ottomans, led by their youthful Sultan, Mehmet II, known to Turks as 'the Conqueror', finally succeeded in capturing the city of Constantinople. However, far from representing the defeat of a glorious empire, the Ottoman victory was more of a final symbolic act. The Byzantine capital was, by this time, merely the rump of a former mighty empire, with a population estimated at no more than fifty thousand.

The city that Mehmet the Conqueror envisaged as his own imperial capital required repopulating – and the Ottoman policy knew no nationalistic exclusivity. The Sultan brought Greeks and Armenians as well as Turks from other cities to assist in the economic resurgence of the conquered city. Churches were restored as mosques were built, and the cosmopolitan character of Constantinople / Istanbul was established from the outset. The various communities had their own specialisms in terms of occupations, and each contributed its own areas of expertise. So, towards the end of the 15th century, when Mehmet's successor, Beyazit II opened his welcoming arms to Jewish refugees from the Spanish Inquisition, he saw it as a natural step in the economic strengthening of his empire. The Jews brought financial expertise and other trade skills that the Ottomans needed. Neither Turkish ethnicity nor Islamic belief were prerequisites for citizenship.

It is a fascinating feature of the Jewish community in Istanbul that most of them trace their ancestry back to the Sephardic refugees who made their home in the Ottoman Empire after the forced conversions and persecutions of the Spanish Inquisition. While Turkish is their first language today, their rituals and music preserve the Judaeo-Spanish dialect known as Ladino, which they brought with them from their homes in the Iberian Peninsula. As an aside, contrary to popular belief, it was Jews and Muslims who were the main target of the Spanish Catholic Inquisitors at that time, rather than Protestants, whose Reformation had barely begun, and certainly not in Spain.

A sub-branch of the Jewish community in the Ottoman Empire was the *dönme*, followers of the 17th century self-styled Messiah, Sabbatai Zevi. This gentleman made himself unpopular with the Ottoman establishment at the time, and he and his supporters had to convert to Islam in order to remain within Ottoman borders. It is said, however, that they maintained their Jewish faith and rituals behind a Muslim façade.

Unlike the Spanish, the Ottomans were, apparently, content to accept the 'conversion' at face value, and refrained from applying unpleasant methods to identify backsliders. Two of the better-known private educational foundations in Istanbul today, FMV Işık and Terraki, are reputed to have been founded by the *dönme* community in Salonika, whence they moved after the population exchanges following the Turkish War of Independence.

Several sources set the number of synagogues in modern Istanbul at twenty-one, with a further eleven in Izmir, and a sprinkling in other Turkish cities. By contrast, modern Thessaloniki, formerly, during Ottoman times, regarded as the largest Jewish city in the world, has three[8]. At that time known as Selanik, the city became part of Greece in 1912. Subsequently, a huge fire in 1917 destroyed much of the city including most of the synagogues and left many of the Jewish community homeless. After the Nazi occupation of Greece in 1942, Jews were rounded up and sent to death camps. The mortality rate is reported to have been 98 percent.

The Republic of Turkey maintained its neutrality for most of the Second World War until the final months. During the war, however, several Turkish diplomats did their best to alleviate the suffering of Jewish people under threat from the Nazi extermination machine. Behiç Erkin was Turkey's ambassador to France from 1939 to 1943. During this period he worked to identify members of the Jewish community who were of Turkish origin, and to persuade the Nazi authorities that they should be repatriated to Turkey. His efforts are believed to have saved thousands of Jews from removal to concentration camps.

Necdet Kent, Turkish Consul-General in Marseilles, is recognised as having put his own life at risk to save Jews from transportation to Nazi camps. Stories are told of how he boarded a train loaded with Jews of Turkish origin bound for Germany, refusing to get off until the Jewish prisoners were allowed off too.

Selahattin Ülkümen perhaps saved fewer souls, but paid a higher price for his humanitarian efforts. As Turkish consul on the island of Rhodes during the Second World War, he worked to have many Jewish families shipped to Turkey to save them from Nazi round-ups. After

---

[8] 'Maven Search', Jewish Web Directory: http://www.mavensearch.com/synagogues/ C3391Y41895RX

Turkey abandoned its neutrality in the last months of the war to side with the Allies, his house was shelled by the Germans and his young wife fatally wounded. He himself was interned in occupied Greece until the war ended.

Undoubtedly there have been incidents in subsequent years where Jewish people have been victimised in local incidents – but for the most part, Turkey, and the earlier Ottoman Empire, have an exemplary record of good relations with the Jewish community, in comparison with their European neighbours. Turkey has at times acted as a mediator in Middle East conflicts involving Israel. There is a free-trade agreement between the two countries, and Israel is an important supplier of arms to the Turkish military.

Prime Minister Erdoğan has a tricky task as leader of a secular, parliamentary democracy with its strategic location on the fringe of the Middle East. Much of his predominantly Muslim electorate undoubtedly sympathises with co-religionist brethren suffering from Israeli expansion (and missiles). Continually fobbed off by Europe in their attempts to gain membership of the European Union, Turkey will inevitably look to form partnerships with more accommodating neighbours. At the same time, Turkey continues to direct its aspirations towards acceptance among the civilised nations of the world – and friendship with the USA and Western Europe is a prerequisite for this. Politics, for the most part, is a business of compromise. Perhaps a little grandstanding on Mr Erdoğan's part in front of his Islamic neighbours abroad and supporters at home is understandable, in the circumstances.

12

Beyond Futility -
Gallipoli Revisited

20 April 2010

One of my first expeditions out of Istanbul was a school trip. I'd started working at a small private high school as a teacher of English. My English colleague and I tagged along with a coach-load of Turkish students and teachers. Our itinerary took in the small town of Çanakkale on the Asian shore of the Dardanelles, the archaeological excavations of Troy, and the Aegean seaside village of Behramkale, alongside another historical site, the ancient city of Assos.

I was really looking forward to seeing the ruins of Troy, but it turned out that Çanakkale was, in fact, the most important destination for us. It was 17 March and the town was buzzing. We stayed overnight in a hotel, rose early on Saturday morning and found vantage points near the town square to watch the parade. There was music and dancing, military bands, students from dozens of local schools regaled in traditional folk costumes – all the ingredients of a major celebration. And what was the occasion? Çanakkale Victory Day.

Well, it's possible that you may not immediately get the significance of this, so let me go on. After the parade, we crossed to the European side of the strait and were taken on a guided tour of the graveyards, museums and battle sites of what we grandsons and daughters of the British Empire know as the Gallipoli Campaign. We saw row upon row of gravestones in neatly kept cemeteries preserving the memory of the estimated quarter of a million young men who died in this tragic side-show of World War I. We climbed to the highest point on the peninsula, Conk Bayırı in Turkish, known in English as the ridge of Chunuk Bair. There we saw the larger-than-life statue of Mustafa Kemal, the Turkish colonel whose success here began his rise to eventual founder and first president of the modern Republic of Turkey.

Nearby, on the ridge whose name is enshrined in the title of a play by New Zealand author Maurice Shadbolt, there is another, slightly smaller monument. No statue adorns it – merely a laconic inscription in English, *'From the Uttermost Ends of the Earth'*. It commemorates the hundreds of New Zealand soldiers who died while capturing and holding, for a brief 48 hours (undoubtedly an eternity to the few who survived) this desolate peak which, it is said, held the key to the entire campaign.

Of course others died too. West Country men, from Gloucestershire and Wales fought and died alongside the New Zealanders . . . and hundreds of Ottoman soldiers fell too, urged on by their command-ers who well understood the strategic importance of Conk Bayırı. They recaptured the ridge on 10 August 1915, and Allied forces never again succeeded in getting so near to achieving their goal, though they re-mained four months more on the peninsula, pouring out their blood on the beaches, the slopes and in the ravines of Gallipoli, before the bitter Thracian winter convinced their commanders that the campaign was a lost cause.

Anyway, I guess you're with me now. You've realised that the futile exercise in human slaughter we refer to as the Gallipoli Campaign, is known to the Turks as the Çanakkale War. They didn't have much to celebrate after the so-called Great War, so they are justifiably proud of their success in defending their homeland against Allied invasion. What concerned me, however, as I toured the trenches, trying to imagine the carnage that had taken place here, eighty years before, was . . . how come the Turks are celebrating their victory on March 18, when we hadn't even got here till April 25?

My first thought was that it might have something to do with the Islamic calendar. After all, the Ottomans continued using the old lunar reckoning based on the Prophet Mohammed's journey to Medina, right up until their final dissolution. But, no – 18 March, it seemed, was 18 March; and 25 April, by anybody's calculation, comes five weeks later, so long as they occur in the same year, which they did, on this occasion: 1915.

What to make of that? So I did a little digging, and it turned out that the Turks, of course, have a very good reason for their choice of dates.

It's important to understand, first of all, what exactly the Anzacs and other sons of the British Empire were doing on that desolate peninsula, some two thousand kilometres from the action on the Western Front. In fact, the situation in France and Belgium had bogged down pretty early on in the war. First Lord of the British Admiralty, Winston Churchill, came up with the idea of supporting Russia to mount a major offensive from the east. Problem was, the only realistic supply route for Russia was via the Black Sea and the Bosporus Straits, which were controlled by the Ottoman Empire, who, of course, were fighting on the German side. So, you take out the Ottomans, open up the Bosporus to Allied traffic, bolster up the Russkies and pincer the Germans and their allies by opening up a second major front on the east. Very neat. And who better to sort out the Ottomans than the Royal Navy, in those pre-air force days, the world's premier fighting force.

Unfortunately, it didn't work. The Ottomans had had fortifications on the Dardanelles for five hundred years, and, with a little help from their German allies, had some fairly serious shore-based firepower at a point where the straits are less than two kilometres wide. They'd also had sufficient warning of the impending assault to lay mines as an extra deterrent. Nevertheless, the British, aided by the French, felt confident of their naval superiority, and sent a force of eighteen battleships plus assorted cruisers and destroyers to force their way through to Istanbul. Despite possessing such imposing names as *Irresistible* and *Inflexible* (and their French equivalents), three battleships were sunk and three more severely damaged. Discretion was deemed the better part of valour, and the Entente navies retired to lick their wounds. The sea approach was crossed off the list of strategies, and Allied thoughts turned to Plan B.

Plan B? You guessed it – a land invasion of the Gallipoli Peninsula aimed at neutralising the Ottoman shore defences so that the battleships could sail through with less discomfort, heave to in front of the Sultan's Palace in Istanbul, and order the Grand Turk and his Sublime cohorts to come out with their hands up. Well, Europeans had been making jokes about 'The Sick Man of Europe' for so long that they didn't expect much serious opposition. Perhaps a little less gung ho jingoism, and some knowledge of history might have resulted in a more realistic approach. It hadn't been that long since the Ottoman army was feared throughout Europe; and while they were no longer threatening to overrun Christendom, they might have been expected to put up stiff resistance to an invasion of their homeland.

Carrying out an invasion from the sea is a notoriously difficult military activity. The Allied forces achieved it at Normandy in 1944, as a result of elaborate planning, enormous investment of manpower, equipment and supplies, huge naval and air support, not to mention the participation of the United States of America. Even so, there were horrific casualties. In 1915 aerial warfare was in its infancy, and naval bombardment seems to have been as much of a curse as a blessing for the Allied troops on the ground. Nevertheless, Plan B went ahead. Regiments of young men from all parts of the British Empire were landed on Gallipoli beaches to face the machine-guns, artillery and bayonets of entrenched and determined troops fighting for the defence of their native land.

Predictably, Plan B was a worse failure than Plan A. A two-day naval engagement was followed by a nine-month attempted invasion. Where the loss of three battleships and around one thousand sailors had been deemed unacceptable, a war of attrition was allowed to continue from April 1915 until January 1916, in which hundreds of thousands were sent to die in inhuman conditions with no realistic hope of success.

Some semblance of justice can be said to have been effected with the metaphorical rolling of heads that followed back in London after the withdrawal from Gallipoli. Winston Churchill lost his prestigious job as First Lord of the Admiralty. The British War Secretary, Lord Kitchener, kept his job, but lost his reputation, and, in fact, died the following year. General Sir Ian Hamilton, overall commander of the campaign, was nudged into retirement, as was General Sir Fredrick Stopford, who is reputed to have slept through the landings at Suvla Bay that he was, in theory, in charge of. The Liberal Government of Prime Minister Herbert Asquith lost its majority and was forced into a coalition with

Conservatives led by David Lloyd George, who not long after, replaced him as Premier.

Little enough consolation for the families of the sons, brothers and husbands who had died; and it is even more dispiriting to learn that, as far as the Turks are concerned, the war had been won before the first Allied soldier set foot on those fateful beaches. The Royal Navy was the number one fighting force in the world at the time, and if they had succeeded in forcing a passage through the Dardanelles, the war, for the Ottomans at least, would have been pretty much over. Turning back His Majesty's battleships reduced the threat to a land invasion, which the Ottoman military backed themselves to repel.

As, in fact, they did, despite the best efforts of the Allied soldiers who fought and suffered above and beyond the call of duty for upwards of eight months. In later years, as the truth of the horror and crass stupidity came out, one positive has been the growth of a sense of nationhood among the former colonies that sent men to fight for the British Empire. For the Turks, of course, the Çanakkale War threw up their one victorious commander, who subsequently went on to lead the struggle to establish the Republic of Turkey from the ashes of the Ottoman Empire. Thousands of pilgrims from 'Downunder' who journey to the peninsula of Gallipoli on 25 April each year, and are welcomed by locals in a spirit of friendship, have cause to remember his magnanimous words:

> *'Those heroes that shed their blood and lost their lives... You are now lying in the soil of a friendly country. Therefore rest in peace. There is no difference between the Johnnies and the Mehmets to us where they lie side by side now here in this country of ours... You, the mothers, who sent your sons from faraway countries, wipe away your tears; your sons are now lying in our bosom and are in peace. After having lost their lives on this land, they have become our sons as well.'*

As an epilogue to the foregoing, I would like to mention an interesting tale I came across recently while reading a novel by the Turkish author, Buket Uzuner. One detail of the Gallipoli campaign that is often mentioned in Allied reports is the fact that the first landings were made in the wrong place. Instead of coming shore on a gently sloping sandy beach, the unfortunate soldiers found themselves facing steep ravines and cliffs. Generally the mistake is attributed to the pre-dawn darkness in which the landings were made (as if navigation were really such an imprecise art in the early 20th century). In her 2002 novel, *'The Long White Cloud'*[9], Ms Uzuner has one of her characters, Ali Osman say:

> *. . . [A]ccording to local legend, Turkish fishermen noticed an unfamiliar buoy moored out near Kaba Tepe and grew immediately suspicious, being already in a wartime state of mind. They reported the incident to police headquarters in Gallipoli, then, that same night, with the help of a few soldiers, moved the buoy fifteen hundred metres north to Arıburnu Cove, a most unsuitable place for a military landing. At the time, there was only one Turk who believed that the enemy might land at the Arıburnu/Anzac Cove, and that was a colonel named Mustafa Kemal. Indicating that even the Turks did not take the signal buoy very seriously at the time.'*

I haven't been able to verify the story, but it's an interesting and not implausible one, it seems to me.

---

[9] Remzi Kitabevi, 2002 (tr. Pelin Ariner)

13

No Mean City

16 May 2010

It was announced well in advance, of course, that Istanbul would be 'European Capital of Culture' in 2010. What I hadn't known was that it would, in fact, be one of three European Capitals of Culture that year, the others being Pécs and Essen.

Now I don't wish to in any way detract from the cultural significance of Pécs and Essen. I am happy to have been given the motivation to find out where Pécs is – and I can tell you (in case you are as ignorant as I was) that it is the fifth largest city in Hungary, and home to the country's largest university. Of course I knew where Essen is. I can't tell you if it is the seventh or the eighth largest city in Germany, but I can assure you that it was formerly one of the country's most important coal and steel centres.

I'm not sure exactly who decides, from year to year, which cities will be designated European Capitals of Culture. However, since the decisions are made by a committee of the European Union, I guess Turks, as non-members, should be grateful that one of their cities made the cut at all.

Nevertheless, the decision having been taken to grace Istanbul with the title, I can't help wondering whether the honour was not a little diluted by including it as a member of what can only be considered a fairly humble triumvirate. If you glance, as I did, down the list of previous title-holders, you will see that such relative metropolitan minnows as Cork, Ireland (2005) and Patras, Greece (2006) were deemed to have no competition in their respective years; while Luxembourg (2007) was given a second bite of the cherry twelve years after its first chomp.

Well, I'm sorry. It wasn't my intention to bitch about other culturally worthy European cities. After all, there's a lot of culture in Europe – undoubtedly enough to provide the gnomes of Brussels with cities for their list into the foreseeable future, even at the rate of two or three a year.

In fact, the spark that ignited this particular chapter was a table I came across which I am appending for your edification[10]. It shows the population figures for Istanbul over a period of 1,677 years. Well, of course, it hasn't been known as 'Istanbul' for all of that time – only for the last 559 years. Prior to 1453, as Constantinople, it was the capital of the Roman Empire for 1,123 years – a title it shared with the actual city of Rome for a relatively brief 146 years, before that city, as is well known, was overrun by barbarians.

You'll notice, as you look at the table, that it hasn't been all beer and skittles for the imperial city over that millennium and a half. Periods of dramatic growth have been followed by equally dramatic periods of decline. Given the exponential growth of the population in the last thrty years, it's not easy to graph the figures in order to convey the fluctuations that took place at various periods of the city's history. However, it's obvious that those numbers want to tell us a story, and so I've decided to help them do it.

One point that should be made at the outset is that the very existence of these figures is a statement in itself. Clearly we would like to set them alongside comparable figures for other major European and world cities but we can't. The reason is, of course, that either the figures don't exist – or the cities themselves didn't. Istanbul/Constantinople has been around for a very long time; and it has been capital of civilisations that have been sufficiently organized and self-aware to be able to compile reasonably accurate population statistics. Excavations being carried out as part of the Marmaray Metro System have found evidence of a Neolithic settlement at Yenikapı, dating back to around 8500 years ago.

---

[10] http://en.wikipedia.org/wiki/Istanbul

Year	Population	Year	Population
330	40,000	1914	909,978
400	400,000	1927	680,857
530	550,000	1935	741,148
545	350,000	1940	793,949
715	300,000	1945	860,558
950	400,000	1950	983,041
1200	150,000	1955	1,268,771
1453	36,000	1960	1,466,535
1477	70,000	1965	1,742,978
1566	600,000	1970	2,132,407
1817	500,000	1975	2,547,364
1860	715,000	1980	2,772,708
1885	873,570	1985	5,475,982
1890	874,000	1990	6,629,431
1897	1,059,000	2000	8,803,468
1901	942,900	2007	11,372,613

The ancient city of Rome is held by some to have attained a population of up to two million at its peak in the 2nd century CE; but declined to a tiny fraction of this after a series of disasters lasting close to a thousand years. It probably didn't reach 100,000 again until the 17th century. It is nigh impossible to find figures for European cities to be able to compare them with Constantinople/Istanbul. London, for example, is estimated to have had a population of 60,000 in the 2nd century CE at the height of its Roman period – but by 500 CE, to have declined to 5,000. Estimates of its population in 1066, when the invading Normans put an arrow through the eye of English King Harold, range from 5,000 to 40,000. It perhaps hit 100,000 when it became the mercantile centre of England in the age of Chaucer, but declined again, and didn't reach

200,000 till Guy Fawkes narrowly failed to incinerate King James I at the beginning of the 17th century.

Paris was probably the largest city in Europe in medieval times, apparently growing to 200,000 in the 14th century, then remaining fairly static until the 16th century. By 1700 it had managed to top half a million for the first time.

Apart from those cities, what can we find? Undoubtedly there were cities in ancient China that were home to very large populations. Estimates for Hangzhou at its peak in the 14th century range from one to two million, and it was probably the biggest city in the world at that time. Moscow is said to have reached 100,000 in the 16th century, before being attacked and sacked by the Crimean Tatars and falling on hard times. Italian stars of the Renaissance, Venice, Naples and Milan, hovered around the magic 100,000 mark in the 16th century, as did Hapsburg Vienna. Madrid hadn't even become the capital of Spain at that stage – the largest city being Toledo, with an estimated population of 65,000.

So let's return to Istanbul, or rather, to the 4th century CE when the Roman emperor, Constantine I decided to establish a second Rome on the site of the small Greek city, Byzantium, on the triangular peninsula at the southern mouth of the Bosporus Strait. Reasons given for his decision are: the new city stood at an important point on the trade routes between east and west; the eastern parts of the empire were more urbanized and civilized than those in the west; the western empire was increasingly under threat, and the wealth of the East allowed it to buy off aggressors as well as hire mercenaries to assist in its defence. Whatever the reasons may have been, it is clear that Constantine was serious about creating a capital city: the population grew tenfold to 400,000 within seventy years of its foundation!

If you want to read a history of the Eastern Roman Empire, you will need to look elsewhere. However, historians seem to agree that there were two 'Golden Ages', under the Emperor Justinian I in the 6th century, and again, after a period of decline, in the 9th and 10th centuries. At this latter time, the Emperor ruled what could still reasonably be considered an empire, with its western possessions stretching through the Balkans, Macedonia, Greece and southern Italy; its armies holding their own and even making ground in the east against the forces of Islam. As

John Julius Norwich, noted historian of Byzantium has claimed, if not for this resistance in the east, Muslim armies would likely have swept into Europe by the shortest route, rather than having to take the longer road, via North Africa and Spain. In that case, the history and culture of Western Europe could well have been very different. It might, for example, have been Christians asking the Muslim government of Switzerland for permission to build a church, rather than the other way around.

Anyway, we can see these two peaks of success reflected in our figures for the city of Constantinople, with the city having a population of 400,000 in 950 CE. Not long after that, however, the tide turned against the eastern Romans. In 1071 the Seljuk Turks defeated the army of the Emperor Romanus Diogenes, sealing the fate of Asia Minor/Anatolia for the next millennium, and inspiring a succession of Popes to launch their crusading hordes into the east. When the zealots of the Fourth Crusade sacked and pillaged the city of their Christian brethren in 1204, the population of Constantinople had fallen to 150,000. Although the Byzantines regained their capital fifty years later, their empire was doomed. When the Ottoman Conqueror, Mehmet II hammered the final nails into its coffin in 1453, the mighty Rome of the East had fewer than 50,000 inhabitants, and the conquest was probably more symbolic than real.

But what happened next? A further slide into an under-populated, godless dark age? On the contrary, we can see from the table that, within little over a century, the population of the new Ottoman capital (whose rulers, incidentally, claimed for themselves, with some justification, the title of Roman Emperor) grew more than tenfold, to 600,000. At the peak of the Empire's power in 1566, the 'Magnificent' Süleiman's dominions stretched from the mouth of the Arabian Gulf to Algeria; from the Persian Gulf to the gates of Vienna in an arc passing the shores of the Caspian Sea, taking in the Crimea and Hungary.

After the conquest, Ottoman Sultans, from Beyazit II on, encouraged the repopulation of the imperial city, and not just with Turkish subjects. Jews and Arabs, fleeing the Inquisition in Spain, were offered safe haven. Greeks were encouraged to return, the Greek Orthodox Patriarchate being allowed to remain in the city, where it can still be found today. Armenian Christians were given the same special status to use their language and practise their religion. We may take such freedoms for granted today – but in the 16th century, Western Europe was rather less tolerant. Apart from Inquisitorial Spain, the French were beginning their religious purification, leading to the massacre and expulsion of hundreds of thousands of Protestants. England may have adopted a less 'final' solution, but Acts of Parliament prevented nonconformists (i.e. to the Church of England) from holding civil or military office, or being awarded university degrees until the Catholic emancipation of 1828. The first English immigrants to North America were, of course, fleeing religious persecution in their homeland.

But I digress. Another glance at our table shows that there was a decline in Istanbul's population after its peak in 1566 – followed by a slow rise until it topped one million around the turn of the 19th century. This certainly reflects the decline in the Empire's fortunes, which resulted in Western leaders' inventing the term 'Sick Man of Europe'. No doubt the glee with which they employed this term was in proportion to the humiliation their predecessors had felt in earlier times when their ambassadors were obliged to learn the Ottoman language and seek the grace and favour of the Grand Turk on his home turf.

Istanbul/Constantinople was still a grand city – the British Consular building, built in 1844, is testament to this, one of the premier postings for a British diplomat of the day. The Dolmabahçe Palace on the European shore of the Bosporus, and a host of other lesser seaside palaces further testify to the city's continuation as a major world city. Nevertheless, its stagnation is especially stark in contrast to the rapid growth of European cities in the throes of the Industrial Revolution. London, for example, grew from a city of one million, to 6.5 million from 1801 to 1901. New York City, still hovering around the half million mark in 1850, had increased tenfold to five million by the beginning of the First World War.

Alongside these figures of enormous growth, Istanbul's figures are unspectacular. However, we can see that the population did increase 48 percent to over a million in forty years to 1897. The exact reasons for this growth can be debated, but one possible explanation has been documented: according to the historian Justin McCarthy, Muslim refugees amounting to ten percent of the population flooded into the Ottoman Empire as a result of ethnic purification and state terror conducted by the Russians as they expanded into the Crimea and the Caucasus. Far from contributing to its economic growth, these homeless, penniless refugees were a drain on a government already struggling to maintain solvency.

From here, further reference to our table will show another fairly spectacular decline in numbers. In the thirty years to 1927, the population declined 36 percent to under 700,000. Correlating this to events in history, we see that, in 1912, Greece, Bulgaria, Serbia and Montenegro declared war on the Ottoman Empire. The First Balkan War broke out, followed by a second a year later. In 1914 Europe exploded into the Great War, in which the Ottoman Empire, after fighting on at least three separate fronts, ended up on the losing side. The consequence of the harsh conditions imposed by the victorious Allies on the Ottoman Empire was the Turkish War of Independence, in which hostilities dragged on for a further three years until 1922. After ten consecutive years of war, it is not surprising that the numbers of Istanbul-dwellers declined.

After the declaration of the Turkish Republic, the city's population began to increase slowly in time with the gradual recovery and economic development of the new nation. Istanbul passed one million inhabitants in the early 1950s, two million in the late 60s, and three million in the early 80s. Since then the growth has been exponential. The figure for 2007 includes the city proper, and doesn't include the wider urban agglomeration. Whichever measure is used, various sources place Istanbul among the ten largest cities in the world. None of these sources, incidentally, ranked even the largest cities of Germany or Hungary in the top fifty.

Of course, size isn't everything. But I can't help feeling Istanbul deserved a 'Cultural Capital' year to itself.

14

Understanding Turkish Politics

18 June 2010

Recently a full-page advertisement appeared in several major Turkish daily newspapers. The ad featured three Turkish Prime Ministers, past and present, under the banner heading: 'Demokrasinin Yıldızları' - 'Stars of Democracy'.

Well, Turkey is a democratic country – and democracy requires that citizens can, within reason, say, and even publish full-page newspaper ads about, pretty much anything they want. However, the fact that someone (or a group of 'someones') felt the need to fund such an ad suggests that democracy itself, and those who uphold it, are not outside the realm of debate in this country. The matter of who these 'someones' are is a question I will return to later.

Turkey is a young democracy. In 2012 it is celebrating its 89th year. Not so young in terms of a human lifespan perhaps, but short enough in relation to the span of human history. The Republic of Turkey was founded in 1923, and the first open national election was held in 1946. In 1950 a rival party was elected to power for the first time. There will be people in their seventies and eighties in Turkey today who may have seen

Mustafa Kemal Atatürk in the flesh – and the occasional nonagenarian who was around at the actual foundation of the Republic.

Compare the time frame with that of France, for example, or the United States, great early leaders in the establishment of republican democracy. A five-year-old French child who witnessed the storming of the Bastille would have turned 100 in 1889 – when Atatürk himself was only eight years old. An American five-year-old present at the funeral of George Washington would have celebrated her hundredth birthday in 1894.

85 years after the US Declaration of Independence, the young republic fought a terrible civil war in which 620,000 combatants and an unknown number of civilians lost their lives. Its territorial borders were still expanding, in theory, until 1959, when Alaska and Hawaii were added to the list of States. In practice, the US Government was still adding to its territory by means of war against foreign nations until 1898, or perhaps even 1945 if you count territories seized from the Japanese after World War II. The Philippines never actually achieved State-hood, but, in fact, only gained independence from the US in 1946. Slavery was finally abolished nearly seventy years after the Constitution set out to 'establish justice … and promote the general Welfare', but institutionalized segregation and disenfranchisement continued into the second half of the twentieth century, accompanied by exploitation of, and violence against African Americans.

Check out the record of France in the years after the foundation of the Republic. A scant twelve years on, Napoleon had overthrown it and declared himself Emperor. After the rest of Europe ganged up and got rid of him in 1814, the French decided to restore their monarchy. That lasted, in one form or another, until it was thrown out in favour of the Second Republic in 1848. French partiality for absolutism and guys called Napoleon Bonaparte resulted in a Second Empire, which lasted from 1852 until the disastrous war with Prussia in 1870. The Third Republic seems to have come into being at this point largely by default, for want of a monarch willing to be restored, rather than from any major desire in France for democratic government. The French are currently into their Fifth Republic, which came into being after the collapse of its anachronistic empire in North Africa and South East Asia.

Clearly getting a modern-style democracy up and running is not an easy matter, despite the simplistic beliefs of guys called George Bush (even well-established democracies seem to have a hankering for dynasties, have you noticed?). Turkey's founder, Atatürk, himself recognized that force of arms might create a nation, but consolidating, developing and maintaining it was a more difficult and ongoing task. Perhaps far-sightedly, he avoided siring any children who might have been a temptation to Turkish dynasticists.

Anyway, to return to the advertisement that began this chapter. The first matter that aroused controversy in Turkey was the fact that the third member of the democratic triumvirate was the current Prime Minister, Recep Tayyip Erdoğan – a man who served prison time a few years ago for supposedly threatening the Kemalist nature of Turkey; whose wife infuriates secular Turks for her insistence on wearing a head-scarf; and who is often suspected of harbouring a secret agenda to return the country to a state of Islamic Shariah rule.

Well, I'm not party to the machinations of high-level Turkish politicians - but I have been around long enough to be able to make certain observations. From 1995 to January 1999, Turkey had no fewer than five Prime Ministers who were either pretty corrupt, pretty self-seeking or pretty old (or some combination of the three). When RT Erdoğan's party took the reins of power in November 2002, the Turkish Lira was valued at around 1,500,000 to the US dollar, down from a high of 1.7 million in 2001. One consolation for investors for the 80-plus percent inflation rate was that interest rates on bank term deposits were that much or higher. Within two years, the rate of inflation had fallen to manageable single figures, allowing Erdoğan's government to delete six zeroes from the Turkish Lira, which is currently hovering around a re-spectable 1.70 to the US dollar.

In March 2003, GW Bush led an anti-terrorist alliance into Iraq, to unearth weapons of mass destruction that the United Nations, in their namby-pamby, liberal wetness, had been unable to find. Leaders of the Western world, for the most part, threw their various weights behind him. 'Crusade' was a word Bush used early on, but realizing his mistake, he became extremely eager to have Turkey's 99 percent Muslim population with him. There was talk of an eighteen billion dollar aid package to reward such loyalty and support. In the end, the Turks didn't go – and there are no doubt many patriotic citizens of the United Kingdom who would wish that their own Prime Minister at the time had been of such an independent mind.

But what about the other PMs in the 'Stars of Democracy' ad? The gentleman on the left of the picture is Adnan Menderes, who became, arguably, the first genuinely elected Prime Minister of Turkey, when his Democrat party won power in 1950. You might say it was a watershed event in the progress of democracy in Turkey – but was the nation ready? The Republic had been founded on principles of secularism. The Muslim religion had been seen as a hindrance to progress and modernization, as a force for reaction – and Atatürk had done his best to pull its teeth and limit its power. The great man, however, had one major advantage over those who followed him into the seat of Turkish power: he didn't have to win elections.

Aspiring political leaders in the post-1946 era of Turkish politics have had to come to terms with the need to win the support of an overwhelmingly Muslim electorate. As a result, many of the measures instituted by Atatürk in the name of secularization, have been undone, or undermined, by subsequent governments. For example, the use of Turkish in religious ceremonies was substituted or encouraged in place of Arabic in the new republic. The stated reason was the general move towards a pure Turkish language to replace the hybrid Ottoman of the imperial elite. It may be, however, that reformers recognized that general unintelligibility, and arcane knowledge limited to those-in-the-know, are powerful factors in the maintenance of a mass religion. As an aside, it would be an interesting exercise to trace the correlation between increasing use of vernacular languages in worship, and the decline of Christianity in the West.

Whatever the reason, Menderes's Democrat Party reinstituted the Arabic version of the call to prayer that sounds five times a day from minarets on Turkish mosques. His government also set up special secondary schools, called İmam Hatip, for the training of imams and preachers. Apart from these sops to the religious faithful however, the Menderes Government presided over a period of rapid mechanisation, industrialisation and economic growth, and is one of only two administrations in Turkey to have won three consecutive elections. It's a little surprising, then, to learn that the end came as a result of a coup by army officers in

1960; and not content with unseating the poor guy, the military leaders actually had him hanged, along with two of his ministers.

I guess it is some consolation for his family (and the man himself, wherever he may be) that his reputation was subsequently restored to such an extent that there are now city streets and parks named after ex-PM Menderes, and even the international airport in Izmir, Turkey's third largest metropolis. It's possible that the soldiers who staged the coup felt they were justified, since it is widely believed in Turkey that the army has the final responsibility for upholding the secular democratic republic. However, there were two further military takeovers at ten-year intervals after the first. Following the last one, in 1980, the junta actually used religion to counter the perceived threat of socialists and increased the construction of Imam Hatip high schools. Turkish politics is a complex business.

The other figure in the advertisement, the guy in the middle, is Turgut Özal. Mr Özal himself was apparently quite a strong Muslim, from a pretty orthodox background. In the 1970s, he had actually stood for parliament (albeit unsuccessfully) as a candidate for the National Salvation Party, an overtly Islamic party, led by Necmettin Erbakan (who was later ousted from the Prime Ministership, and banned from politics, by 'peaceful' military intervention, for his excessively Islamic bent). Surprising, then, that Mr Özal was one of the few politicians favoured by the military leaders of the 1980 coup, despite also having been undersecretary to the deposed PM, Süleiman Demirel. He served as deputy PM to General Kenan Evren, the leader of the coup, then became PM when his Motherland party won a majority after democracy was restored in 1983. For better or worse, Özal is credited with having brought capitalism to Turkey. Under his leadership, the country was opened to a flood of imports, the process of privatisation of state assets was begun, and a 30 year period of hyper-inflation got off to a flying start - the Turkish Lira depreciated by 1400 percent against the US dollar from 1980 to 1988. A chequered career, to say the least!

As all good Christians know, there are sins of commission, and sins of omission, so perhaps it may be interesting to consider which Turkish political figures are absent from the 'Stars of Democracy' ad. Clearly the salient absentee is Mustafa Kemal Atatürk. Well, perhaps it could be argued that, whatever his credentials as military leader, reformer and statesman, he isn't especially notable for his commitment to democratic elections, so let's leave him aside. However, it's also noticeable that no other leader of the Republican People's Party (CHP) got into the picture either, despite its being recognised as the heir to the Atatürk legacy. But maybe that's debatable. The military leaders of the 1980 coup, who also saw themselves as upholders of the Atatürk 'Way', actually banned the CHP from participating in politics – and it stayed that way until 1992. Since its re-emergence on the political scene, CHP has been conspicuously unsuccessful – this lack of electoral success finally resulting in the internal ousting recently, of its leader of eighteen years, Deniz Baykal.

In the end, then, dazed and confused by the apparent impossibility of making sense of all this, I decided the only smart thing to do was to check out who had actually funded the insertion of that full-page ad in the Turkish dailies. Well, there at the bottom of the page was the acronym SDP, and a web address: www.sivildayanismaplatformu.org, so I checked it out. That was a month or so ago, and the website was covered with ads for various Islamic institutions and events – clearly, you'd have to think, the public face of an organization with major religious interests. Then, as I was finishing this chapter, I decided to check the site again, and behold ... not an ad to be seen, nor the slightest hint of anything religious. Weird, man! Why would you suddenly clean off all the paying ads from your website? Unless, perhaps, you were concerned that curious people like myself might think you had a secret agenda.

Well, who knows? Democracy is a word that can cover a multitude of sins. The German Democratic Republic (East Germany) was not particularly noted for upholding the freedoms and rights of its citizens. In the Democratic Republic of the Congo (formerly Zaire) where the Second Congo War has been raging for twelve years, 5.4 million people have allegedly died, making it the world's deadliest conflict since World War II. The occurrence of rape and other sexual violence has been described as the worst in the world, and the DRC's people have the world's lowest per capita GDP, according to the IMF.

I have no intention of comparing Turkey to either of the foregoing manifestly undemocratic regimes. There is no doubt in my mind that Turkey's present government, like most of its predecessors of the past sixty years, was democratically elected. But democracy is a fragile flower. It needs nurturing – and it can be easily poisoned. I have seen, in my own country, organizations funded by wealthy individuals, or small groups thereof, hiding behind a façade of democratic good intentions in order to push their own agenda of self-interest. Again, I have no quarrel with the choice of those three worthy gentlemen as 'Stars of Democracy'. But something about that full-page ad made me nervous at the time – and the feeling hasn't gone away.

15

Genocide, and the
Procession of History

15 July 2010

There was an interesting exhibition in Istanbul recently – a collection of paintings by an artist called Faruk Kutlu. Not that the works themselves are likely to turn the art world on its head, but the title caught my eye: *'Kafkasya'dan Sürgün'* – in English, *'Deportation (or Exile) from the Caucasus'*. It interested me because I'd recently visited Sakarya, a small city not far from Istanbul, and people there told me that their ancestors had come from the Caucasus region. I'm irresistibly fascinated by these little historical mysteries, so I had to check it out.

It turns out that representatives of the Adygeyans (which is apparently what the Circassian people of the Caucasus call themselves in their own language) have, for some time, been lobbying the Russian Government seeking an apology for an alleged genocide that took place in the 1860s. 'Dammit,' I hear you say. 'This word genocide is going to lose its meaning if it gets bandied around so frequently and lightly' – but I have to say, this one is definitely worth a look.

The Soviet Union, which collapsed in 1991, was heir to the domain of the Russian Empire, officially dated from 1721. By the second half of the 19th century, under Tsar Alexander II, Russia had built the third largest empire in the history of the world, and as we all know, its religion was Eastern Orthodox Christianity. Well, like most generalisations, that's only part of the truth. In fact, the expansion of the Russian border to the south was largely at the expense of central Asian and Caucasian states, which, at the time, were overwhelmingly Muslim.

The policy of successive Russian monarchs had been to 'discourage' the Muslim religion in the interests of civilisation, Christianisation and Russification. Perversely, the Muslim inhabitants of the Caucasus chose to reject the invitation to become part of this Orthodox Russian civilisation, and their resistance lasted from 1817 to 1864. The intervening struggle is variously known as the Caucasian War, the Russian Conquest of the Caucasus, and, apparently, the local Muslim population even had the temerity to call it the Holy War! But in the end, the result was pretty much as you would expect: the big guys beat the little guys, and the price exacted from the little guys was in proportion to the time and inconvenience they had put the big guys to.

What actually happened at this point is, of course, not easy to ascertain. Circassian sources claim that 400,000 of their people were killed and around 500,000 were forced to leave their homes and seek resettlement in the neighbouring Ottoman Empire, many of these refugees dying on the journey, or later in the crowded, insanitary conditions in which they were obliged to live on arrival. Russian sources are understandably less specific on details, but the matter of mass deportation is beyond dispute, as is the fact that Muslim populations within the expanded Russian Empire became minorities in areas where they had previously been the majority.

At this point, I want to turn my attention from the micro- to the macro-, and to introduce a political concept known as 'The Great Game'. You are probably aware that the 19th century saw the beginning of a period in history often referred to as the Age of Imperialism. The major European nations (including Russia) were engaged in the process of empire-building, just as some formerly powerful empires were in the process of disintegration. Key aspects of the imperialism business were: maintaining the balance of power while seeking to grab as much territory as possible for your own empire, and at the same time, limiting the growth of the others.

No doubt you are also aware that India was the 'Jewel in the Crown' of the British Empress, Victoria; and of course, Vicki and her ministers were not amused to see that jewel threatened by the southward expansion of the Russians. 'The Great Game' is the name given to the conflict and rivalry between the British and Russian Empires for control in Central Asia. The 'game' became increasingly serious from the 1850s, when oil began to assume major importance as an economic resource. Political 'game' it may have been considered by some, but in reality, it was played at great expense in money and human life. Take as example the three Anglo-Afghan wars fought between 1839 and 1919. It's almost enough to make you feel sorry for the Afghans. But that's another story.

Running parallel to, and occasionally overlapping this 'game' were the power plays related to 'The Eastern Question'. This was another driving force in the policies of the European Great Powers during the 19th century and up to the end of the First World War. Essentially, the question can be put thus: When will the Ottoman Empire finally disintegrate, and who will get all the good bits when it does? As noted above, all the European empire-builders were keen to benefit from the Ottoman collapse; but at the same time they were equally keen that their rivals should not.

Once you grasp these relatively simple principles, a lot of the otherwise confusing activities of the European empire states, not to mention events unfolding in apparently distant unrelated places, become more intelligible.

Take, for example, the Crimean War. The Charge of the Light Brigade was no doubt a marvellous example of the incomparable bravery and discipline of the British fighting man. But what on earth was he doing over there fighting a war on Russia's back doorstep for nearly three years? Well, in fact, he was part of a British strategy to keep Russia iced up in its frozen wastes and prevent it from gaining access to the warm waters of the Mediterranean. In the 1850s, this strategy required bolstering up the Ottomans and helping them defend their realm.

Go back, however, a mere 26 years to 1827, and you would find the warships of Britain, France <u>and</u> Russia fighting together to destroy the Ottoman navy off the coast of southern Greece. At that time, it suited the European powers to encourage and then support Orthodox Christians to unite in a nationalist struggle and declare the independence of the

Greek peninsula. We can guess that the British were keen to have a compliant puppet state in the eastern Mediterranean, but what was in it for the Russians? Most likely there was some deal going on – you help us out here and we'll try to work something out for you over there. Turn a blind eye to what you're doing to the Muslims in central Asia, for example? Incidentally, you might want to ask how those Russians got their ships into the Mediterranean to participate in the battle. That's the trouble with history – you answer one puzzling question and it raises several equally troubling new ones.

But I refuse to be sidetracked. Our subject is genocide, and its euphemistic little sibling, ethnic cleansing. The Greek peninsula had been part of the Ottoman Empire for centuries, and its population had large Muslim and Jewish elements. In fact, at this point, it will be worth our while to take a look at the composition of the Empire. The Ottomans were a ruling elite, for sure with their origins in the Turkish migrations from central Asia, but, by reason of conquest, long residence and intermarriage, considering themselves cosmopolitan, and even (dare I say it?) European. They regarded themselves, with some justification, as the legitimate heirs of the Byzantine Roman Empire; the Sultan's mother would almost certainly have been a Byzantine princess, or Bulgarian, or Russian, but assuredly not Turkish. Their language, although based on Turkish, had a large admixture of Persian and Arabic. Their empire included a wide range of ethnic groupings, religions and languages, and interestingly, they didn't really try to impose uniformity.

The Ottomans recognised four *millets* (nations) within their boundaries, based primarily on religion. Islam was the state religion, but this group included Arabs and Kurds, as well as Turks. Christians and Jews were 'people of the book', so they were permitted to retain their religious practices and languages, especially the local varieties of Christianity, Greek Orthodox and Armenian. They, with the Jews and the Muslims, made up the four *millets* of the empire.

What happened at the time of the Greek 'War of Independence' was a forerunner of what was to follow as the Ottoman Empire fell apart. We could say that the repercussions have continued to be felt into our own times. For their own ends, the European powers encouraged nationalist sentiments among the Christian subjects of the Ottoman Empire. They then presented themselves as protectors of the Christian minorities when Ottoman authorities, not unreasonably, came down hard on separatist movements within their borders. One side effect of the Greek War of Independence was the killing of rather a lot of Muslim civilians, whose families had been living on the Greek peninsula for centuries.

Similar scenarios were played out in Bulgaria and other parts of the Balkans in the later years of the 19th century, as Russia and the geriatric Austro-Hungarian Hapsburg Empire encouraged, also for their own purposes, (Christian) nationalist movements to rise up and throw off the chains of Ottoman hegemony. In fact, Muslims were still being slaughtered in the Balkans, and refugees streaming from Bulgaria into Turkey long after the demise of the Ottoman Empire, right up into the 1980s.

The fledgling state of Greece also took the opportunity to expand its territory at the expense of the beleaguered Ottomans. The important trading city of Selanik, birthplace of Mustafa Kemal Atatürk, and reputedly home to the largest Jewish population in Europe, was taken by the Greeks in 1912. Not long after, a catastrophic fire wiped out most of the Jewish and Muslim parts of town, and you will look hard to find a mosque or a synagogue in the modern Greek city of Thessaloniki.

When the First World War ended, the victorious vultures descended in force on the body of the dying Ottomans. It has been argued that the punitive damages imposed on Germany at that time contributed to the rise of Hitler and thence to the Second World War. Under the terms of the Treaty of Sevres, the Ottoman Empire was not merely to be punished; it was to be dismantled and the pieces given into the hands of outsiders. For our purposes, the most significant event was the landing of a Greek army on the Aegean coast of Anatolia backed by the guns of warships from the European victors of the 'Great War'.

What ensued was a three-year war, during which Christian inhabitants of the region at first welcomed their 'liberators' and many Muslims were killed, followed by a successful counter-attack by the newly formed Turkish nationalist forces. Needless to say, some revenge was undoubtedly exacted by the now victorious Muslims. The end result was a forced population exchange in which Muslims and Christians, who had existed side by side in relative harmony for centuries, were forcibly relocated: the Christians of Anatolia being sent to mainland Greece to be replaced by Muslims going the other way.

It's a sorry tale, isn't it! But history is history, and you can't turn back its relentless tide, however much you may wish to. Before we finish, however, let's return to the other theatre of conflict we were discussing earlier – the expanding southern borders of Russia. Of course, as the British well knew, the Great Bear would not be content with merely adding a few central Asian state-lets to its empire. A major goal was always access to the Mediterranean. Clearly the Bosporus Straits would be ever problematic, so another option was to drive a channel though eastern Anatolia, again, at the expense of the moribund Ottomans. Fortunately a pretext was available in the form of the Christian Armenians, who could be incited to rebellion, then offered 'protection' in the form of a Russian invasion to help them set up a nationalist state from which any inconvenient Muslims could be ethnically cleansed (though the term was not invented till later, of course). Again, we may suspect that Armenian independence would have been short-lived, or nominal.

However it was, Armenian nationalists in eastern Anatolia were enthusiastic about Russian support, and ready to create 'incidents' which would encourage Russian intervention on their behalf. The Ottoman government, for their part, had a clear example, in the Caucasus, of what was likely to happen in the event of the Russians gaining control. Whatever happened to the Armenian *millet* in 1915, and undoubtedly it was a tragic event, it needs to be remembered that, as always, there are at least two sides to the story. The Ottoman Empire was fighting for its life in a major war on at least three fronts. And, in an analogous situation, as the present-day Russian government has pointed out with respect to the Caucasus deaths, the pre-revolutionary Russian Empire was a different entity.

There is a short story, 'The Whale', penned by the New Zealand author, Witi Ihimaera, which ends with an elderly Maori leader weeping over the bodies of a pod of beached whales. The whales can be seen as symbolising the old culture and traditions of his people, the indigenous race of New Zealand, whose way of life has been irretrievably lost. 'No wai te he?' the old man cries. 'Who is to blame?'

Temple of the Roman Emperor Trajan on the acropolis of ancient Pergamum

Funeral at Armenian Church, Kadiköy, Istanbul, 2011

Memorial to New Zealand Anzacs on the ridge at Chunuk Bair (Turkish Conk Bayiri)

The author on the summit of Mt Nemrut with statues of the Commagene King, Antiochus I

Tomb of a Venetian knight on the floor of a mosque in Northern Cyprus

Modern Turkish students visiting their Ottoman past, Süleimaniye Mosque, Istanbul.

16

Cruelty and Mercy - Righting the Wrongs of History

18 August 2010

I was doing a little shopping in my local area of Istanbul the other day and I dropped into a small hardware shop. There was an elderly chap behind the counter, and I guess he doesn't get a lot of customers, so he was keen to chat. As usual, I was picked as a non-native as soon as I walked in the door, and he wanted to know where I was from. Like most Turks I have met, he was happy to come across a foreigner, especially one who knew enough Turkish to hold up the other end of a conversation.

Something I have started doing recently in these situations, after exchanging a few pleasantries, is to ask my new acquaintance where <u>he</u> is from. Turks get around a lot, and you can't assume everyone you meet in Istanbul is native to the metropolis. Even if he was born there, a Turk will probably still identify strongly with his '*memleket*', the place where his family came from.

Well, it turned out that the gentleman was from Bulgaria, as are quite a number of Turks you will come across. It seemed a good opportunity to ask when and why he had come to Turkey. In response, he held out his left hand and directed my gaze to the thumbnail – or the place where you would normally expect to see a thumbnail. 'They pulled it out,' he said simply. 'This too,' he said, indicating a large rough scar on his forehead. He didn't take off his shoe, but he added that the big toe of his left foot had been crudely amputated with an axe. 'They wanted us to change our names,' he explained, 'and I am proud of my Turkish name.'

So he'd come to Turkey, along with more than 300,000 other Bulgarian Turks who fled anti-Muslim persecution in the late 1980s, leaving behind houses and most worldly possessions.

Now I want to make it clear here that he wasn't complaining, and his tone wasn't bitter. He had made a new life for himself and his family in Turkey, and he seemed content. He was merely responding matter-of-factly to my questions. I did a little subsequent reading on the subject, and, to be fair, this persecution of Turkish Muslims took place under the old Communist regime, which was overthrown not long after. The new government restored rights and freedoms to Muslim Bulgarians, and many of the refugees chose to return from Turkey. I visited Sofia briefly in 2004, and saw a historic mosque in a prominent location. An important landmark on the shores of the Golden Horn in Istanbul is a 120 year-old Bulgarian Orthodox church, so these must be good signs.

I saw another good sign in my Turkish newspaper a day or two later. Two hundred members of an extended 'Süryani' family were celebrating a reunion in their *'memleket'*, the southeast Turkish town of Mardin, whence they had fled to various countries because of terror and violence. At a colourful traditional ceremony, they reopened the doors of the seven-hundred-year-old mansion they had inherited from their forebears.

Well, of course, such an event begs several questions, among them: What actually happened to make these people leave in the first place? And shouldn't someone be held accountable for that?

Maybe someone should – but unfortunately, it's not always easy to find a person, or government that can be persuaded, or forced, to shoulder the blame. The present government of Russia is understandably reluctant to accept responsibility for atrocities carried out by Imperial Czarist Russia. Republican Turkey regrets events that took place under the Ottoman Sultans, but shares this reluctance to assume guilt. Perhaps, if the United Kingdom became a 'United Republic', they might be able to distance themselves from some of the worst excesses carried out in the name of the British Empire. You can't help feeing a little sorry for the modern Brit sometimes.

But I know these are not matters to be treated lightly. Historical wounds leave deep scars, and national pride thrives on the memory of past injustices. We New Zealanders know how difficult it is, with the best intentions, to right the wrongs of history. Historical facts themselves can be elusive will-o'-the-wisps, even when the history is less than two hundred years old. How much more difficult, then, in a land which witnessed the dawn of history itself!

You can commonly see, in Turkey today, agricultural implements and conveyances that hark back to the very earliest days of civilisation. They are not much used nowadays. Mostly they are to be seen on display in gardens or antique shops: ancient stone olive presses, primitive sleds and carts with spoke-less wooden wheels attached with a peg to a revolving axle. Such wheels were introduced in the third millennium BCE prior to the invention of spokes, but have been in use in Turkey within living memory.

Did you get that? Let me just run that by you again: the third millennium BCE! We're talking four to five thousand years ago here, long before any Turk set foot in the region now known as Anatolia. And, we could also add, for that matter, quite some time before any Greek. History goes back a long way in this part of the world – the practice of writing is generally accepted as having emerged simultaneously around 3000 BCE in both Egypt and Mesopotamia. Turkish schools kids are required to memorise a bewildering list of civilisations that succeeded each other over a period of four thousand years until the Ottomans hammered the last nail in the Byzantine coffin with their conquest of Constantinople in 1453.

Historians and archaeologists are not always 100 percent certain where these various peoples came from before they established their kingdoms and empires in this ancient land. The period of six hundred years after 1300 BCE, sometimes labelled the 'Ionian Collusion', you will find elsewhere referred to as the 'Anatolian Dark Age', marked by invasions and conquests of the mysterious 'Sea People'. Nevertheless, we can be fairly sure of two things. First, human nature being what it is, there would have been a fair amount of bloodshed and slaughter of the vanquished by the victors. Second, the nature of invasions being what it is, there would also have been a considerable amount of assimilation and accommodation taking place in the aftermath, such that elements of the earlier culture would have mixed with elements of the new to produce a new synthesis.

Well, we can find plenty of examples of the bloodshed and slaughter, and I have touched on some of the more recent ones here and elsewhere, so it is not this on which I wish to focus. Rather, I want to speculate a little on the assimilations and accommodations that must have taken place.

One fact historians do agree on is 1071 CE as the date of the battle that saw the beginning of the Turkish conquest of Anatolia. The Byzantine army was defeated, the Emperor taken captive, and the Turkification/Islamicisation of Anatolia begun. But how many Turks actually entered Anatolia at this time, and what percentage did this represent of the total population of the area? What happened to those predominantly Christian, Greek-speaking local inhabitants? Were they slaughtered? Did they move en masse to friendlier lands? Were they forcibly converted, along the lines of later Christian inquisitorial methods? Or did the majority of them survive, gradually adopting the customs and practices of their new overlords, while intermarrying with them and passing on some of their own ways and traditions?

I make no claim to expertise in this complex area. To this day, Turks and Greeks squabble over who invented baklava, dolma (dolmades), şiş kebab (souvlaki) and Turkish (Greek) coffee. Nevertheless, it's easier to imagine the Turkish bath having developed from its Roman predecessor, rather than being dismantled and carried on horseback from the steppes of Central Asia. It is undeniable that the imperial mosques of Ottoman Istanbul derived their architectural inspiration from the soaring dome of Hagia Sophia. The rakı and fish which characterise a Turkish night on the town clearly owe more to Mediterranean than Mongolian geography.

But what of that Byzantine Empire overrun by marauding Turks in the late Middle Ages? The name 'Byzantine' itself, as I have pointed out before, was never used by those imperial people to describe themselves. In their eyes they were Roman, direct descendants of the founding twins nourished by a she-wolf on the banks of the Tiber. The Turks themselves recognise this in the word they use (*Rum*) to refer to the Greek-speaking peoples of Anatolia. But there's the rub, you see. The prevailing opinion in Western Europe was that real Romans spoke Latin; and for sure they weren't Christian. Once the Pope started trying to resurrect the Roman Empire in the West, albeit in holy guise, there was no room for another competing one in the East. The Eastern Romans suffered in the eyes of the West because they had adopted too much of the local culture, despite, of course, having conquered (and maybe even having killed some of) whoever had been there before them.

Then there is the matter of Christianity which, simplistic Western views notwithstanding, was born and raised in the Middle East and Anatolia. Evangelism is a tricky business, made easier if you can find ways of melding your new religion with the culture and traditions of the prospective converts. I remember seeing a mural in a small Roman Catholic church in the backblocks of northern New Zealand. The depiction of the Saviour was noticeably brown and Polynesian in appearance. No doubt those early missionaries were able to draw an analogy with the Maori demi-god Maui, son of an earthly mother and the immortal guardian of the underworld, whose rebellious streak and supernatural powers brought great benefits to the lives of the mortals with whom he lived.

Christian visitors to Turkey often visit a humble building near the modern town of Selçuk, said to mark the spot where Jesus's mother lived, having been brought there by the apostle John after the traumatising death of her son. Hard to know for sure, of course, though the Pope himself, on more than one occasion, has given credence to the story by visiting and praying at the site. More verifiable, however, is the long tradition of mother goddesses in the Aegean region of Anatolia. The Phrygian goddess Cybele mated with another semi-deity, Attis, who later reportedly cut off his own genitals, inspiring a cult of eunuch priests (a more certain way of enforcing celibacy rather than merely relying on self-restraint – perhaps the Roman Catholic hierarchy should be looking into that). Cybele seems to have morphed into the popular Greek goddess Artemis, with connections to the moon goddess Selene, the Roman goddess Diana, and the Carian goddess Hecate. Who's to say those early Christian evangelists didn't find going with the local flow sometimes mutually beneficial?

What I'm suggesting here is that the twin processes of conquest and assimilation have been going on in this part of the world for millennia, and it's an impossible task to separate and isolate the individual components of the culture and people that exist in Turkey today.

Take as another example the archaeological excavations at Kültepe, some twenty kilometres from the modern Turkish city of Kayseri. The site is also known by its ancient name of Karum Kanesh, where Kanesh was a city inhabited by local Hittites from around 2000 BCE, and Karum, a satellite trading outpost of Assyrian merchants from Mesopotamia. Clearly the two peoples learnt each other's tongues, and the visitors even taught their hosts the cuneiform alphabet in which have been preserved the earliest surviving inscriptions in the Hittite language.

This practice of allowing traders to set up a permanent trading base adjacent to a major city evidently continued until recent times. The city of Constantinople / Istanbul was enclosed within the ancient city walls until little more than a century ago. Across the Golden Horn, the settlement of Galata/Pera was the home of Genoese and Venetians in the Middle Ages, and later, of European Levantines; and where the embassies of foreign powers were located until the new Turkish Republic chose to site its capital in Ankara. The Christian districts of Pera and Kadıköy (Chalcedon) on the Asian shore of the Bosporus retain a more open attitude to alcohol consumption and related entertainments than is customary among Muslim communities.

We seem to have travelled a long way from my local ironmonger from Bulgaria, and I confess I have led you on a rather labyrinthine journey: to Mardin and Russia, the United Kingdom and New Zealand, Egypt and Mesopotamia, Greece and Rome, Selçuk and Kayseri, before returning at last to Istanbul. Was there a point to it all? It's easy to imagine the violent loss of a thumbnail and a toe arousing anger and even hatred against the perpetrator of the action, especially if the violence could be associated with matters of nationalism, religion and ethnic identity. The line separating anger and hatred from bomb-throwing and vicious revenge is easily crossed, and escape from the cumulative circular spiral of grievance and vengeance is difficult. Unscrupulous seekers of power know this and use it for their own ends. In the final analysis, as the poet William Blake said, cruelty and mercy both have a human heart, and what use to make of that heart is ours to choose.

17

The Turks are Coming!

20 September 2010

I come from a rugby-mad country. New Zealanders love sport in general. We are lucky to be born in a country where nature is kind – the weather is mild and there is plenty of open space. Children have the opportunity to choose from an unlimited range of physical activities, but the Number One choice is, and always has been, rugby football.

When I was a kid at primary school, there were two choices for a boy: play rugby, or be considered a 'poofter' (if you don't know the word, look it up). These days, there are far more options available, and NZ has produced champions in almost every kind of sport, from lawn bowls to boxing; from speedway racing to yachting; from field hockey to middle distance running, rowing, kayaking and putting the shot. The NZ men's soccer team competed in the 2010 FIFA World Cup, finishing unbeaten in their group, ahead of Italy. The men's basketball team recently defeated the Russian and Chinese teams to win the Stankovic Cup at a major tournament in Guangzhou, China.

However, NZ has a small population, and it is not possible to compete consistently with the top countries in the world in every sport. From time to time a world-beating player or team appears, but we may have to wait many years to achieve the same success again. This is true in every sport – except rugby. Rugby is king of sports in New Zealand,

and the honour of the nation is carried on the broad shoulders of our national rugby team, the All Blacks. When the All Blacks play against another country, it is far more than a mere sporting event – the result may be the cause of nationwide rejoicing or mourning.

But not all matches are of equal importance. Apart from New Zealand, there is one other country for which rugby is the number one sport. And I use the word 'sport' here advisedly. The other country is South Africa, and the rivalry between these two can be compared to the televised bouts of 'World Wrestling Entertainment', except rather more serious and infinitely less theatrical. When the All Blacks emerged victorious from a match last year with the South African Springboks, the NZ coach, Graham Henry, had this to say about his team: 'These are the guys I would want to have beside me in a war!' And I'm sure he wasn't joking. When it comes to smiling, Henry would make the Turkish football coach, Fatih Terim, look like a stand-up comic.

Speaking of the 'Imparator' and the Turkish national football team brings me back to my main point. I read an article in my Turkish newspaper recently, in which the president of the Youth and Sports Development Council announced that they were intending to introduce rugby to Turkish youth – and my heart skipped a beat. The rugby-playing nations of the world have managed to keep their game out of the hands of the Turks – until now! It could be the beginning of the end. My pick is that, if the Turks really get into the game, they'll have a fair chance of getting their name on that William Webb Ellis trophy by 2019. 'Yeah, sure!' I hear you say. But listen up . . .

If there's one nation on Earth that knows about war, it's the Turks. If you had to choose a group of guys to have on your side in the event of one, you could do a lot worse than pick a bunch of Turks. Look at a list of the largest empires in world history. The Ottoman Empire comes in at Number Five. If you're prepared to relax your definition of 'Turk' a little to include the Mongols, they're actually in second spot; and obviously you don't build an empire of that size without doing a fair amount of fighting. In fact, if it hadn't been for some pretty desperate resistance by Hapsburg forces in 1529 and 1683, the Ottomans might well have conquered Vienna and made major inroads into the heartland of Europe.

A glance back further into history reveals that this Ottoman threat to Europe was no surprise. Before the Turkish emir Osman founded the Ottoman dynasty in 1299, Turks had been fighting as hired war-riors in the armies of most major regional powers for several centuries. The Persians, Egyptians, Byzantines, Venetians, and even, interest-ingly (more recently and somewhat surprisingly), the United States of America[11], have all availed themselves of Turkish mercenaries at one time or another.

In the seventy years from 1853 to 1923, as the Ottoman Empire col-lapsed and finally disintegrated, its people fought no fewer than seven major wars, beginning with the Crimean War, and ending with the War of Independence, out of which emerged the modern republic of Turkey. Of course, apart from the last named war, there weren't a lot of successes for the Turks to boast of in that period – but for sure, they weren't short of fighting practice. If the British hadn't swallowed their own rhetoric in the 19th Century about the Ottoman Empire being the 'Sick Man of Europe', they might have been a little less sanguine about their chances of success in the Gallipoli invasion of 1915. The Turks may have been short of technology, but they remained dangerous foes when backed into a corner.

Coming up to the present day, there is still universal compulsory military service for all male citizens of Turkey. Furthermore, it is not mere token training. The majority of young men serve fifteen months in the armed forces, and many of them see action in the east of the country in the on-going struggle with Kurdish insurgents.

However, Graham Henry's remarks notwithstanding, rugby is a sport – a fact attested to by the intention of the International Olympic Committee to include it in the Games from 2016. So let me return to my other reasons for thinking that Turkey may well become a force to be reckoned with.

Turks love football. In fact, the word 'love' doesn't really do jus-tice to the emotions that football arouses in the Turkish breast. It's my opinion that the rivalries between supporters of Turkish football clubs have their roots in the factional riots originating in the chariot races of Ancient Rome, which periodically laid waste the city of Constantinople (old Istanbul, of course). Not only do supporters of competing Turkish clubs not mingle during a match, but large numbers of uniformed police

---

[11] The First Barbary War 1803: http://en.wikipedia.org/wiki/Tripoli#Contemporary_era

armed with automatic weapons stand guard to ensure they do not come to blows, or worse.

However, the football that inspires this fanaticism is not rugby. It is, of course, the 'poofter' variety played with a round ball, indulged in by the misguided majority of the world's nations, in which players hurl themselves to the turf in paroxysms of agony when an opponent approaches within spitting distance. Turks are, actually, quite good at this pansy version of football, though their results on the world stage tend to be somewhat erratic. One of the chief reasons for this could be that Turks are not very good at feigning injury, and are more likely to stoically refrain from showing weakness in competitive situations.

Nevertheless, the Turkish national soccer/football team did finish third in the 2002 FIFA World Cup – a creditable performance that put them in the same company as international powerhouses, Brazil and Germany. According to that newspaper article I mentioned earlier, the Turkish Sports Development people have recognised the need for large skilful athletes in fielding a rugby team. Wrestling and handball are two important sports in Turkey, and they suggest that similar talents are useful in rugby too. Further, they are focusing on the recruitment of players two metres in height, 110 kilograms in weight, capable of running 100 metres in under 13 seconds.

One thing that struck me when I first came to Turkey was how many short men there were. However, in a country of seventy million people, there is a wide range of body shapes and sizes, and a Turk by the name of Sultan Kösen recently entered the Guinness Book of Records as the world's tallest man. In the World Basketball Championships (a sport unsympathetic to normal-sized human beings), held in 2010, the Turkish Men's team finished runners-up to the USA. We may safely assume that they won't have a problem finding fifteen guys large enough to foot it with the man-monsters of the other rugby-playing nations.

I want to finish with a brief anecdote from my early days in Turkey. When I first came to this country, I took up a position teaching English in a private high school in Istanbul. My students were of no great intellectual stature, but they were cheerful, outgoing and enthusiastic, keen to initiate a 'green' foreigner into the intricacies of Turkish culture. One morning, after our lesson ended and we broke for lunch, a group of sixteen-year-old lads offered to demonstrate for me a popular playground game known as 'Long Donkey'. Later, of course, I understood that this 'game' is totally off-limits in Turkish schools, but at the time I was keen to learn about local customs, and reluctant to hurt the feelings of my pupils. So the lads proceeded to clear a space in the classroom by moving the desks and chairs around, and the game began.

Let me explain how 'Long Donkey' is played. Two teams are chosen. The numbers don't really matter, but let's say, on this particular day, there were seven a-side. A coin is tossed and one team becomes the 'donkey'. The leader of the team braces himself in a standing position facing a wall, and the rest of his team bend over and grasp the lad in front in a long, scrum-like formation. The other team, meanwhile, withdraw themselves as far away from the 'donkey' as possible, and conduct themselves as follows: the first player takes a running jump, aiming to land himself, with as much force as possible, on the back of the 'donkey'. The object, as you may guess, is to collapse the 'donkey', or, failing that, to remain on its back so that, when the next player follows, the combined weight is increased.

All players in the jumping team take their turn, and, if the 'donkey' is collapsed, a point is scored, or not, as the case may be. Team roles are then reversed, and the game continues until the players tire of it, someone is seriously injured, or the police are called, whichever comes first.

Well, luckily I was able to terminate my first experience of 'Long Donkey' before we went that far – and, fortunately, before any of my Turkish teaching colleagues came on the scene. But ever since that day, I have been wondering what would happen when and if Turks were able to combine their love of football with their warrior tradition and their enthusiasm for 'Long Donkey'. It seems that the rugby world is about to find out.

18

Art for God's Sake - Gentrification in Istanbul

18 October 2010

There has been a lot of doomsday talk in and about Turkey recently, particularly in the lead-up to, and as a result of the recent referendum on the constitution. The essence of the talk seems to be that Turkey is lurching inexorably back into the Islamic world, and eighty-seven years of secular, Western-oriented progress, instigated by the revered founder of the Turkish Republic, Mustafa Kemal Atatürk, is being systematically unravelled. The most recent evidence of this retrogression, so the doomsayers tell us, is the violence that took place in the inner-city district of Tophane, where a gang of thugs, armed with clubs, knives and pepperspray (an interestingly modern addition to traditional armament) set upon citizens peacefully attending the opening of several art galleries in the area.

Well, let me say at the outset that I do not, in any way, condone this kind of street violence. It is unconscionable that citizens attending such an event, folks you would normally expect to be peaceful, intellectual, even a little other-worldly, should end up in hospital with knife wounds and concussion while going about their lawful business. Art gallery owners, victims, and their friends and families are rightly angry about what happened on 21 September 2010.

I must admit, there are times when I despair of the world, and feel that the end of civilisation as I have known it, is assuredly at hand. Usually, however, the feeling passes, I get matters back into some kind of perspective, and remember that life, on the whole, is pretty comfortable for me, and others in the circles I generally move in. So let's step back from the events of that Tuesday night, and try to take a broader view.

First, then, there is the matter of street violence. Of course it's a nasty matter, and, for those immediately affected, extremely traumatising. However, a scrap that sees five people treated at hospital for relatively minor injuries, and seven taken into police custody, hardly qualifies as an apocalyptic event. In fact, on the microcosmic level, if two of the injured had not been foreign citizens, and those set upon had not been well-heeled attendees of an art gallery opening, the fracas would very likely have received no media attention at all, and certainly not have made international news. Worse things happen, I'm sure, on a pretty regular basis, in any major Western city - and Istanbul has a population of more than twelve million.

On another level, however, there is an important insight into Turkish society provided by this event. Ten years ago, in April 2000, hundreds of supporters of the English Football club, Leeds United, arrived in Istanbul to attend a UEFA Cup match with the local side Galatasaray. Prior to the match, a group of Leeds fans managed to get themselves into an altercation with some natives, with the tragic result that one Englishman was stabbed to death, and another ended up in hospital with a serious knife wound.

Again, you cannot condone the violence, but as a visitor to Turkey, you should take the trouble to look into the local character. Turks are famed for their friendliness and hospitality to visitors. They are generally slow to anger, as anyone knows who has witnessed the anarchy on the roads of Istanbul, and the relatively few incidences of road-rage. On the other hand, it is well known that, once a fight does break out, there is no backing down. Carrying an offensive/defensive weapon is not uncommon, and bloodshed is a predictable result. Every year I go to the main police security HQ in Istanbul to renew my residence and work permit. As we enter the premises, of course, we are x-rayed and searched. An interesting variant on what I was used to, however, is the desk to which you can surrender your firearm, where it will be looked after until you have completed your business. For this reason, local bystanders tend to do all they can to prevent an argument escalating to violence. As a general rule, it's better to avoid getting into a fight with a Turk if you can do so with honour preserved on both sides.

Which brings me to the next level of my analysis: the reasons for the conflict in Tophane. I read an article in the Turkish Airlines in-flight magazine 'Skylife', commenting on the transformation taking place in the historic area of Tophane. Gentrification is a relatively recent phenomenon in Istanbul, but it has long been common elsewhere, and the stages of the process are well known. The writer of the article describes how the gentrification process spread from the fringes of the neighbouring, already developed districts of Cihangir and Beyoğlu. The arty middle-classes were lured by the opening of a large new city art gallery, Istanbul Modern, in a huge old warehouse on the Bosporus shore. They began to see the potential of an area characterised by run-down, but attractive nineteenth century buildings with low rents or price tags. A new kind of resident moved in; art galleries, antique shops and up-market charcuteries opened, local small businesses found their incomes increasing, and rents began to skyrocket. The city council sees urban renewal taking place at someone else's expense, and at the same time, the potential to increase property taxes. It happens everywhere, and everyone's a winner, right?

Unfortunately, wrong. The inevitable corollary of an influx of new residents is the displacement of the old. The old residents, needless to say, are mostly poor with no voice to make themselves heard in the corridors of power. And anyway, what is their argument? You can't hold back progress. Money talks. If you can't pay the new rents, you'll just have to move somewhere cheaper – generally to some soulless outer suburb where services, facilities and public transport are scarce. Add to that, the Turkish concept of 'mahalle': the inner-city neighbourhood with an identity created by inhabitants whose families have lived there perhaps for generations; whose children have attended local schools; whose small businessmen mostly live in the area, are on first name terms with their customers and have a vested interest in supporting the local economy. Residents of the *mahalle* know each other, and know when a stranger turns up. They help bring up each other's children, are jealous of the reputation of their neighbourhood and for the most part, police themselves. Well, it's not just a Turkish thing, of course. The same spirit existed in Western cities too, in the past, until it was largely swept away by urban renewal and gentrification.

This, of course, is the point I want to make here. '*Tophaneliler*' (old residents of Tophane) see their neighbourhood being invaded en masse by new breed of neighbour who cares little, if at all, for the old ways. They feel themselves being pushed out, and perhaps feel some natural resentment. The resentment can easily turn to violence when sparked by an insult, real or imagined: wealthy new-comers drinking and socialising loudly on streets where formerly this was not the done thing; a word of appreciation directed at a pretty young neighbourhood lass . . . It's not hard to imagine a likely scenario. We can acknowledge the reasons for it, at the same time as we condemn the violence.

The thing about Turkey is that these processes that we have observed elsewhere, are vastly complicated by the sheer age and complexity of the society that exists here. A little uphill, and west of the Tophane district stands one of Istanbul's most famous landmarks – Galata Tower. The tower was built in 1348 as part of the fortifications of the Genoese citadel of Galata. The Genoese had been granted special rights by the grateful Byzantine Emperor after helping to win back Constantinople from the Latin invaders who had set up shop there after the forces of the Fourth Crusade, supported by Genoa's rivals the Venetians, had besieged and conquered the city.

When the Ottoman Sultan, Mehmet I decided it was time finally to add Constantinople to his dominions, Tophane was one of the places he chose to site cannons with which to bombard the city walls. The name Tophane, in fact, means 'cannon foundry', and the old Ottoman foundry remains one of the distinctive buildings in the area today; though it now serves a more peaceful purpose as the Culture and Arts Centre of Mimar Sinan Fine Arts University. The foreshore of Tophane was the place where cargo ships and passenger liners berthed; and before that, had for centuries been docking for warships of the Ottoman Navy. We can imagine the kind of activities that existed in streets back from the waterfront, and the kinds of people who inhabited them.

Two other historic buildings on the foreshore of Tophane are the Nüsretiye Mosque, and the mosque of Kiliç Ali Pasha. Interestingly, the former, built in 1826, was designed by the architect Krikor Balyan, of a well-known Armenian Istanbul family, members of which served as Imperial Architects to six Ottoman Sultans. The older of the buildings was designed by Mimar Sinan (the Ottoman 'Christopher Wren') and built in 1580 to the order of a gentleman whose name we may translate as Admiral Ali 'The Sword'. Despite being an Admiral of the Ottoman Navy, he was apparently born in Italy and went originally by the name of Giovanni Dionigi Galeni. Captured by the Ottomans in 1536, he was put to work as a galley slave, before converting to Islam, and rising through the ranks to end his career as Admiral of the Fleet.

Why am I telling you this, you may ask. Merely to illustrate the fact that getting a handle on what's going on in this part of the world is a complex business. Everyone knows the Ottomans were Turks and they slaughtered Armenians – yet here we have a family of Armenians designing some of the most important imperial buildings (including mosques) and, one must assume, being well rewarded for their time and trouble with money and status well into the 19th century. And the Ottoman Navy, scourge of Christian Europe in the 16th century, commanded by an Italian, who must surely have had ample opportunities to escape long before reaching the lofty rank of admiral.

Events in the late 19th and early 20th centuries irreparably altered the fabric of society in Istanbul, and Turkey as a whole. What was formerly a polyglot mix of peoples, with large populations of Jews, Armenians and Greek-speaking Orthodox Christians, European businessmen and diplomats, has ostensibly become a much more homogeneous community of Turkish Muslims. Yet this apparent homogeneity is misleading. Turkishness itself is an elusive concept, imposed on a diverse and divided population in the 1920s to save what remained of the Ottoman heartland.

The Turkish republic, founded in 1923, was a pre-industrial, largely rural state with a shattered economy and a population of around thirteen million. By 1950 this had grown to twenty million, of which 75 percent still lived in small villages. In the sixty years since then, the population has grown to 75 million, and the ratio of rural to urban-dwellers has almost exactly reversed. Two inevitable concomitants of this growth have been: a huge influx of rural poor into the cities, especially Istanbul; and the rapid appearance of a large urban middle class.

Returning, then, to the point whence we began our odyssey here, the events in Tophane on 21 September last year can be seen as symptomatic of the tectonic changes taking place in the society of modern Turkey. There is a dynamism evident for all to see, in the mushrooming of modern shopping complexes, the spectacular development of transport infrastructure: motorways, airports, underground rail; and the rapid growth of the private health and education sectors, especially universities. At the same time, conservative elements from villages and small towns are more in evidence in the large urban centres; denizens of traditional inner city neighbourhoods are coming into contact with the new middle classes; and inevitably there will be conflicts of interest.

Governing a country as internally diverse as Turkey is no easy task – as the CHP (Republican People's Party) is finding, in its attempts to become a credible opposition. To be Republican is one thing; to be a party of the People, quite another. Every democratically elected government of Turkey since the first free election in 1946 has had to compromise between the secular ideals of the Atatürk revolution, and the religious beliefs of the majority of voters. Compromise, however, is the essence of politics – and the ability to compromise on issues of national importance, the mark of a mature democracy. It's been thirty years since Turkey had its last military coup, and the likelihood of another seems increasingly remote. That has to be a healthy sign.

19

Those Terrible Turks!

21 November 2010

A mong the surprises that I experienced in my first year of teaching English in Turkey was calling the roll and finding that one of the students was named Genghis. Well, I have to admit that was after I'd begun to get my head around the idiosyncrasies of the Turkish alphabet, and realised that's how we write the word spelled 'Cengiz' in Turkish. Anyway, there he was, a slightly overweight fifteen-year-old, with nothing much to distinguish him from his respectably uniformed classmates – Genghis!

Now, of course, I think nothing of it. I have worked with and taught several more Genghises, and suffered no physical harm at their hands. I have had colleagues and students, to all intents and purposes, quite normal, well-adjusted human beings, despite carrying the name Atilla. Kubilays and Timurs have passed through my classes arousing no more interest than if they were so many Michaels or Tylers. Nevertheless, my initial experience of shock, or at least surprise, illustrates an essential disjuncture between the world-views of the peoples of Western Europe and Western Asia. Clearly, an educated, law-abiding, middle-class Turkish couple choosing to name their new-born son Genghis, are unlikely to have in mind the same picture of a bloodthirsty barbarian chieftain leading his marauding hordes out of Central Asia that the name conjures up in Western circles.

What I want to explore here is the thesis that Western views of Turkey have been shaped by historical and societal events going back at least a millennium and a half and continuously reinforced by subsequent events, and by religious and political leaders for their own, sometimes questionable, purposes.

I'm taking, then, as an arbitrary starting point, the activities of one, Atilla the Hun, who terrorised the Western and Eastern Roman Empires in the 5th century CE. This legendary character headed an empire that extended well into Western Europe. His military forays took him through Germany into France and Italy, and threatened the twin capitals of Rome and Constantinople. Atilla's origins are not entirely clear, but certainly the Huns emerged from Central Asia, and may have spoken a Turkic language. Undoubtedly there is a long-standing association, in European minds, of Turks with mayhem, rapine, and generally uncivilised, anti-social activities.

For some reason, this association does not seem to extend to Arabs, despite the fact that the armies of the Prophet swept through North Africa and into Spain in the 7th century CE, establishing an empire that stretched from Spain to India. Perhaps it is because Europeans recognise the debt we owe to Arab scholars who preserved the writings and wisdom of the classical world, which later fuelled the European Renaissance. Or perhaps it is that the rise of the Seljuk and Ottoman Turks established them as leaders of the Muslim world, relegating the Arabs to a minor role in international affairs. Perhaps too, the European mind, for some centuries, considered it unnecessary to distinguish between Turk and Arab, finding it convenient to tar both with the black brush of Islam. In recent years, with rising fears in the West of cross-cultural clashes and axes of evil, the focus has tended to be on the adherents of Islam rather than on Arabs, who have arguably contributed more to the negative image of Muslims in the US and Europe.

Whatever the case, it was the Turks who bore the brunt of Western Europe's fear of and antipathy towards the Muslim religion, which seems to have emerged strongly in the 11th century. It was in 1096 that Pope Urban II initiated the First Crusade – an army (or two) of Christians from Western Europe who set off on the sacred task of defending Christendom from the Muslim 'invaders', and liberating the Holy Places (Jerusalem etc) from their clutches. As usual, there is debate amongst historians as to the exact reasons for this and subsequent waves of Crusaders that launched themselves eastwards.

In the first place, there was certainly an appeal addressed by the Byzantine Emperor Alexus Comnenus to the Pope in Rome for his help in fighting the Seljuk Turks who had recently defeated the Eastern Christians in a major battle, and begun serious incursions into Syria, Palestine and Asia Minor. While it may seem at first attractive to imagine brother Christians helping each other against a common (heathen) enemy, in fact, there was little love lost between the Eastern and Western churches. It had been only forty years since the final schism in 1054, which firmly established their mutual incompatibility.

Secondly, it is certainly true that Western Christians were at least partially motivated by the belief that the Holy Places of their religion had fallen into the hands of unbelievers. It is also true, however, that these places had been in the hands of Arab Muslims for more than four hundred years. Why the sudden concern, we might ask? Undoubtedly the Turks posed a threat of a different kind. The Eastern Christians had managed to maintain a buffer against Arab Islam, and Constantinople had withstood their attempts to conquer it. The existence of this Eastern barrier had protected Europe from Muslim invasion at a time when it would have been particularly vulnerable. The Arabs were obliged to take the long way around, via North Africa, into Spain, by which time, we may imagine, their supply lines were somewhat stretched. Suddenly, however, in 1071, the Byzantines had been heavily defeated by a Muslim Turkish army – it could have looked like the thin edge of a new wedge.

Third, this event happened at a crucial time in European history. European Christendom was a fragile, relatively new bud. The Carolingian Empire of Charlemagne that had emerged in the mid 8th century had fallen apart by the middle of the 9th. A century later, the Pope had found a new hero in a German king by the name of Otto, and begun grooming him to be temporal ruler of a new Holy Roman Empire. However, Europeans at that time had no real concept of themselves as such, and Western Europe was divided into numerous warring feudal states. The Seljuk Turks, then, might be seen as a convenient threat whose existence could be used as a means of uniting Europeans against a common enemy. In fact, they were not ignorant barbarians, as their art, architecture, literature and philosophy show. Educated Westerners know the verses of Omar Khayyam, through the translation of Edward FitzGerald, and the Sufi philosophy of Mevlana Rumi. But religious leaders, and seekers of political power are not always interested in the whole truth, and a timely war can help paper over internal divisions and generate a unity of spirit and purpose, as Margaret Thatcher and the Bush father and son can verify.

So, the Seljuk Turks became the Pope's bogeyman to terrify Western Christians into laying aside their internecine squabbles and uniting under the banner of true religion. They were assured of finding a place in paradise in return for fighting the good fight against the Saracens, pagans, infidels and Ishmaelites who were polluting the Holy Places. It may also be that the Holy Fathers were a little envious of their Eastern Christian brethren who had retained a temporal empire to go with their spiritual dominion, and saw an opportunity to bring them down a peg or two. Certain it is that the forces of the Fourth Crusade in 1204 took time on the way to engaging the Muslim foe, stopping over long enough to besiege, conquer and loot the Christian city of Constantinople. That city remained in Western hands until the Byzantines were able to retake it some fifty years later, by which time much of its fabled wealth had been relocated to Italian cities, and Byzantine power had been seriously diminished.

Genghis Khan, on the other hand, deserves much of his bad press. His armies swept through Central Asia and the Near East in the early 13th century. After his death, his son Ogedai continued the thrust into Hungary and Poland. Whether or not the Mongols were Turks is a moot point, but certainly they were not Muslims at this time in history. Muslims in fact suffered at least as much as Christians from Mongol depredations – Persia (modern Iran) was invaded and much of Islamic-Arabic civilisation was destroyed. Ironically, it may well be that Genghis and his Mongol hordes thus assisted Christendom by facilitating their re-conquest of the Iberian Peninsula.

Timur, (Tamerlane), another Central Asian warlord, and another open to several interpretations, is in fact less known in the West, perhaps because he caused more damage to Turks, fellow Muslims and Hindus than to Christians. The Ottoman Empire was on the rise in the late 14th century when Timur and his armies defeated Sultan Beyazit, creating an inter-regnum and a serious blow to the emerging power in Anatolia and the Balkans.

Nevertheless, all these events and characters have been lumped together in European folk history to create an image of 'The Turk' that, by the 16th century had crystallised into a heathen figure of darkness and savagery. I haven't personally counted them, but I have it from a source[12] I have no cause to question, that there are thirty-five references to Turks in Shakespeare's plays, all of them referring to a fearsome threat in the East. Indicative of the confusion in European minds is the play 'Tamburlaine', written by Christopher Marlowe in 1587. Marlowe's protagonist (Timur, as discussed above), undoubtedly had a far more recent connection to Central Asian Turkishness than did Beyazit, but English theatregoers were encouraged to cheer Tamburlaine's defeat and humiliation of the Ottoman Sultan. Of course, the reign of Kanuni Süleyman (1520-66), known in the West as Suleiman the Magnificent, marked the pinnacle of power of the Ottoman Empire, with his armies achieving dominance through North Africa, the Middle East and Eastern Europe as far as the gates of Vienna, while his navy controlled much of the Mediterranean. The existence and power of the Ottoman Empire at this time were a major spur to the ocean-going explorations of Western European nations, who needed a safer route to the far East. So perhaps western Europeans were prepared to support a genuinely heathen Turk against a more civilised Ottoman on the principle that 'my enemy's enemy is my friend.'

The Ottomans were not, in fact Turks, in any genetic sense of the word. It had been nearly five hundred years since their ancestors had conquered the Byzantine army at Manzikert. Modern DNA analysis suggests that the genes of those Seljuk invaders had been thinned by intermarriage with the indigenous inhabitants of Asia Minor. Ottoman Sultans filled their harem with toothsome young lasses from the lands they had conquered, and by the 16th century, Süleiman's Turkic blood would have been well diluted. To be Turkish, in fact, did not convey very high status in a cosmopolitan empire whose citizens included Christians, Jews, Arabs and Persians. European use of the title 'The Grand Turk' to

---

12 'Open Democracy', Gönül Bakay: http://www.opendemocracy.net/arts-multiculturalism/article_2273.jsp

refer to the Ottoman Sultan, and the name 'Turkey' to refer to their dominions, likely sprang from an attempt to belittle and diminish a people
they, perforce, had to respect and fear. Atatürk, the founder of the modern Turkish republic, had his work cut out for him in his attempt to
forge a unifying identity from those who remained after other national
groups had split off and gone their separate ways.

However, I am jumping ahead of myself here. We are still back
around the turn of the 17th century, but the tide was turning in European
affairs. The Ottoman Empire was still a major force, and would remain so until its final demise in the First World War. However, new
military technology and training, professional armies and the ability to
work together against a common enemy were beginning to give an edge
whereby rare and infrequent victories over the Ottomans became more
regular and eventually the expected norm. Fear of 'The Turk' began to
be replaced by a curiosity and interest in things Turkish. As trade and
diplomatic relationships increased, wealthy Westerners began to imitate
and adopt aspects of Ottoman/Turkish art and culture – it was known
as 'Turquerie', and was particularly fashionable from the 16th to the 18th
century. By the 19th century, as the Near East became increasingly accessible to the Western traveller, 'Orientalist' artists began to portray
Ottoman culture as colourful, exotic and sensual, qualities to be seen in
the work of the French painter Ingres who was particularly keen on de-
picting 'odalisques' – less exalted members of the Ottoman harem whom
Ingres is most unlikely to have seen, particularly in the unclothed state
in which he was fond of showing them.

From quaint, sensual and exotic, it was but a skip and a jump for
Europeans to accept the diagnosis of the Ottoman Empire, generally
attributed to Czar Nicholas I of Russia, as 'The Sick Man of Europe.'
As the 19th century wore on, the major European powers became more
confident in using the Ottomans in their power games, now attacking,
now supporting, as they manoeuvred around to ensure that each got
the best deal when the 'Sick Man' finally expired. The Ottomans, and
thereby the Turks, came to be seen as enfeebled, dissolute and corrupt,
and fair game for Western empire-builders as they jockeyed for position
in the new world that was emerging. It is entirely understandable. The
once-feared enemy had become vulnerable, and it was too tempting to
mock and belittle now that the threat had passed.

Nevertheless, it can be dangerous to start believing your own propaganda. I have written elsewhere on the Gallipoli campaign in 1915, and the war that led to the emergence of modern Turkey in the 1920s, so I don't intend to repeat the details here. It is pretty clear, though, in retrospect, that the British and their Allies in the First World War seriously underestimated the ability of Turks to defend their own shores from foreign invasion. It is also clear that certain influential figures in the military misrepresented 'The Turk' to the British public. Again, I dealt somewhat harshly with Winston Churchill in an earlier piece, so I'm leaving the poor man alone this time. There is another gentleman, however, who does deserve a little attention. T.E. Lawrence (of Arabia) was undoubtedly a scholar and a gentleman (at least on his father's side, though he apparently adopted his mother's family name, for reasons we needn't go into here). Nevertheless, it does now seem that some of the more titillating passages in his 'Seven Pillars of Wisdom' may have been influenced by his quirky sexual proclivities, which, it is said, included paying a military colleague to administer beatings to him.

Coming up to more modern times, I recently watched 'Midnight Express', that 70s classic film of a young American's experiences in a Turkish prison. Well, I guess, it has come to be recognised as a somewhat exaggerated and distorted representation of Turkey and its justice system. Billy Hayes, the real-life victim, and the scriptwriter who turned his book into a screenplay, have subsequently admitted that fairly major liberties were taken in the making of the film. Perhaps there is no significance in the fact that the owner of MGM studios at the time was an Armenian-American, but you can't help wondering. I have to say that, as I watched it, I couldn't escape the feeling that, perhaps, US authorities, concerned at the activities of young citizens abroad in those days, might have had some input, in the interests of scaring them into being more careful. After all, Billy Hayes confessed in the film, if only to his father, that his aim was to make money by selling hashish back in the USA. I don't know what the law says in Turkey or America, but in New Zealand, if you are caught in possession of more than a certain amount of a particular illegal substance, there is an assumption that you are a dealer.

Well, Turks get a bad press; I guess that's what I want to say. Some of it, perhaps they deserve. Show me the perfect country and I'll move there tomorrow. But a lot of it they don't deserve, and I've tried to show

how our attitudes in the West have been shaped by ignorance, and some-times, even by deliberate distortions. Turks themselves are not wholly innocent in the unfortunate image they have abroad. I recently asked some Turkish friends if Genghis Khan and Atilla the Hun were Turks. 'Probably not,' was the unanimous answer. And perhaps, to be fair, those names are not as common in classrooms as they once were. But sabre-rattling is an activity much-loved of nationalists everywhere, and the ignorant are easily exploited by unscrupulous politicians. In the end, the only defence is true knowledge. Seek it out!

20

Gifts from Turkey

18 December 2010

In the previous chapter, I attempted to show that Western Europe tends to have a rather stereotyped and historically questionable view of Turks that colours their dealings with the modern Republic of Turkey. I'm not trying to argue for any cultural identity to replace the misconceptions, and certainly not to suggest any kind of cultural superiority. Nevertheless, when I have aired these ideas in public, they have provoked a response in some circles, and a question I have been asked is: What have those Turks actually given the world?

'The problem', a friend suggested, *'is that Turkey was never part of the Enlightenment, and didn't produce a Madame Curie or any significant medical or scientific discovery that benefited mankind that has any resonance with people in the West.'*

Well, it's a fair question, I guess, if a little unkind, and I'm grateful for it because it gave me a theme for this chapter – and new inspiration doesn't always come easily. An apparently simple question, however, does not always elicit a simple answer. I guess, if there is a unifying theme to this book, that would probably be it. One question often leads to another, and yet another, and before you know it, you have a 2,500-word rave!

At the outset, then, it's important to define our terms. Who, exactly, do we mean when we say 'Turks' or 'Turkey'. As I tried to suggest in the previous chapter, Westerners tend to have a rather confused concept of Turkishness – and even 'Turks' themselves would have difficulty defining the word. In an earlier chapter I discussed the concept of 'Greekness', another term that tends to be confused in the mind of the ordinary Westerner-in-the-street. Do we mean the citizens of the modern nation we call 'Greece'? Or do we mean the citizens of the loose confederation of city-states we choose to call 'Ancient Greece'? Do we include the 'Greek' speaking, 'Greek' Orthodox citizens of the Byzantine Empire? In both of the latter cases, the majority of the people concerned actually lived on the 'Turkish' side of the Aegean Sea, so you see the nature of the problem.

Atatürk, the founder of the modern Turkish Republic, is often quoted as saying: *"Happy is the one who says, 'I am a Turk.'"* It wasn't just rhetoric. The Ottoman Empire was falling apart, with major assistance from the European victors of the First World War. Nations were being created from the ethnic groups that formerly made up the Empire: Greeks, Bulgarians, 'Yugoslavians', Armenians . . . In order to save at least the Anatolian heartland of the Empire, Ataturk was obliged to create a national identity that could be fought for. So, if you wanted to live in the new country, and you said you were a Turk, that's what you would be.

There is an analogous situation in New Zealand, where a proportion of seats in the Parliamentary House of Representatives is reserved for members of the indigenous race. There are no blood or DNA tests, or examinations of skin, eye and hair colour; nor is there any compulsion. Essentially, if you identify with the concept of Maori-ness, say you are Maori, and have your name entered on the Maori electoral roll, the law of the land will consider you Maori.

So, the first definition of 'Turk' we can consider would be 'a citizen of the modern Republic of Turkey.' If we accept this narrow sense of the word, then there was no 'Turk' and no 'Turkey' prior to 1923. However, I suspect that is not what the questioners have in mind. It's certainly not a definition that would be accepted by the Armenian genocide activists, who insist that modern Turkey is responsible for the sins of the Ottoman Empire. So we need to look for something else.

One of the points I was trying to make in the previous chapter was that the present-day citizens of modern Turkey have very little in common with the Turkic tribes that emerged in waves from the steppes of Central Asia from time immemorial, despite what Turkish school kids are taught in their history lessons. The connection is probably comparable to the relationship between the modern citizens of the United Kingdom, and the Anglo-Saxon migrants who invaded 'England' in the 5th century CE. In fact, given that the existing religion and culture in Anatolia were stronger, the Turkish cultural influence was very likely less. Nevertheless, I will resist the tempting diversion of asking what those Anglo-Saxon tribesmen (and women) gave the world. I will merely direct the curious reader to a wee poem, much loved by my Scottish kinfolk, entitled 'Wha's Like Us?' – in which thirteen key inventions of English daily life are shown to have been actually invented by Scotsmen[13].

Anyway, I don't want to be seen as avoiding the issue, or using cheap debating tricks to turn the tables on my interrogators. So, let me address myself to what is probably the spirit of the question: What did those Turkic invaders from the steppes give the world? And I hope I may be allowed to include the Ottomans here. If modern Turks are expected to shoulder responsibility for the sins of their predecessors, it seems unreasonable to deny credit for their virtues.

Well, let's start with the Central Asian Turks, since those are the ones who started the problem in the first place. If they'd just stayed where they were, Europeans would've been a lot happier and more comfortable. They could have just kept on fighting each other in their petty little wars and not had to bother about uniting against a major outside threat. If nothing else, it might have saved them from having to take collective responsibility for the present-day debts of the Greeks and the Irish. Certainly they wouldn't have had to fight the Crusader Wars; and they could have continued travelling overland to Asia, so they might never have had to sail across the Atlantic Ocean and maybe they'd never have 'discovered' America. In which case, Native Americans would probably have been a lot happier too – and maybe quite a number of Africans and their descendants could have continued to live undisturbed in their benighted ignorance.

---

[13] 'The Capital Scot': http://thecapitalscot.com/pastfeatures/likeus.html

But enough of the negatives. Are there any positives? Well, yoghurt, for a start. You knew that one, didn't you! What about the stirrup? Bet you didn't know the Turks brought that out of Central Asia and it didn't reach Europe until the 7th century CE. However, once it arrived, it apparently caused great upheavals. Some historians have even claimed that it led to the birth of feudalism[14]. And on a related subject, take the composite reflex bow, a handy little weapon that allowed mounted horsemen to shoot arrows to deadly effect. Despite its small size, it is claimed to have a fifty percent greater range than a longbow, with less effort required to bend it. Of course, its advantages faded with the introduction of firearms – but then, gunpowder itself came from China! I'm not going to claim shish kebab for the Turks, since 'kebab' apparently originated in Persia – but the word 'shish' is indisputably Turkish. The making of felt from wool is another debatable one, since its origins are lost in the mists of time – but the Turks certainly had it early, and used it to good effect in making tents and clothes to withstand the rigours of winter on the steppes. Then there is Turkish delight, which I will return to later; and the Turkish bath . . .

Let's move on to the Ottomans, rulers of an empire that lasted from 1299 till 1923 – a five-century regime that compares favourably in duration with pretty much any other empire you could name. In fact, if you care to include their predecessors, the Seljuks, whose empire extended from the Central Asian steppes to the shores of the Aegean, you could add at least another two centuries to that. Hard to imagine that anyone could rule anyone or anywhere for that length of time without leaving some kind of cultural mark. However, specifics are called for, so let's delve in . . .

I have to confess that one thing that has prevented me from really familiarising myself with the growth and spread of Islamic culture, has been its sheer complexity and multifariousness. My eyes tended to glaze over as I read of Sassanids and Abassids, Samanids and Ghaznavids, and other clearly important '-ids' who succeeded each other in controlling 'the East' for centuries after the armies of the Prophet emerged from the Arabian desert.

However, if you would like a grotesquely over-simplified nutshell version of what was going on, you could do worse than think in terms of

---

[14] Check out 'The Great Stirrup Controversy': http://en.wikipedia.org/wiki/Stirrup#The_stirrup_in_Europe

a Turco-Persian culture, which, from the 8th century, began to take over from the Arabs and spread its influence from Bengal to Asia Minor, absorbing, moulding and synthesising, as it grew, the languages, sciences, literatures and technologies with which it came in contact. Initially Turks were apparently brought in by the dominant Persians to serve as soldiers and palace guards, but eventually they themselves rose to dominate their one-time masters.

Now I would like to draw back a step from this breathtakingly outrageous oversimplification to consider what happened when these Turks entered the world of Arabic-Persian Islam. Undoubtedly they saw much that was new and impressive, and they learned to take on board the ways of their adoptive culture. We may further imagine that the Turks who were brought in for martial purposes were predominantly male. From this we may suppose that, if they were not to die out in a generation, they must have found spouses from among the resident population. Another step of logic will tell us that the Turkic blood would quickly have mixed itself with that of the Persians and others who dwelt in this enormous area.

Recent studies suggest that the DNA of present-day inhabitants of Anatolia resembles that of peoples throughout the Mediterranean area. It seems that the Turkic tribes of Central Asia made a barely detectable contribution to the genetic make up of the modern day 'Turk'. This is more or less as we would expect if we accept estimates that the late Byzantine population of Anatolia was around twelve million, and the inflow of 'Turks' from the 11th century is unlikely to have exceeded one million[15]. Nevertheless, those 'people of the West' whom my questioner is representing would, I am sure, want to include the Ottomans within their definition of 'Turks' so I'm going to run with that. In so doing, I want to return to that Turco-Persian culture we were discussing in the previous paragraph-but-one.

One thing is very clear if we take the trouble to look at the historical development of Islam as a world religion. It began with the Arabs in what is now Saudi Arabia, but within a century it had spread beyond their control, and by the 13th century, it was the dominant religion of several empires extending into Central Asia, India, West Africa, Malaya and parts of Europe. Without wanting to go into the details of how it

---

[15] http://en.wikipedia.org/wiki/Turkish_people

happened, we know that, by the early 16th century, the Ottoman Sultan had assumed, as one of his many titles, that of Caliph, political leader of the Muslim 'nation'. The language of the Ottomans, the ruling elite of the Empire, was an amalgam of Persian and Arabic on an essentially Turkish base, written in a modified version of the Arabic alphabet. The Ottomans were the last manifestation of the Turco-Persian culture, until their demise at the end of the First World War.

What I'm getting at here, in case you were wondering, is that it's not terribly easy to identify which of the multitude of gifts to world civilisation that spring from that Turco-Persian Islamic culture can be directly attributed to 'Turks'. Coffee is a case in point. It seems it was first consumed as a drink in a form we might recognise in Mokha, Yemen, in the 15th century, from where it spread throughout the Middle East, and thence to Europe via the Venetians towards the end of the 16th century. Well, who was in control of the Middle East in those days? And who were the Venetians trading with? The Ottomans (Turks) of course. We tend to associate the tulip flower with the Netherlands – but in fact it was first cultivated in the Ottoman Empire, and the word itself comes to us from Persian by way of Ottoman (Turkish).

Tin-glazed pottery originated in Persia in the 9th century and reached its peak as an art form in the Ottoman Empire (Iznik, in modern Turkey), from where it passed into Europe, emerging as Delftware in Holland in the late 16th century. The Sufi order of mystical Islam was not a 'Turkish' development, but its greatest figure, Mevlana Rumi, although born in Persia, lived most of his life in the Anatolian city of Konya, at that time (13th century) capital of the Rum Sultanate of the Seljuk Turks.

If you are ever in the Turkish city of Edirne (former Adrianopolis) near the border of Turkey and Greece, I advise you to visit the mosque complex of Sultan Beyazit II. The 'külliye', as it was called in Ottoman Turkish, is now a museum. From its construction in the late 15th century, it included a medical school and hospital, part of which was given over to treatment of the mentally ill. Contemporary documents show that such treatment included soothing sounds such as the playing of music and the running water of fountains, and manual tasks such as basket weaving. As an interesting comparison, the Royal Hospital of Bethlehem in London served as the city's 'lunatic asylum' well into the

19th century. It was notorious for the brutal treatment of inmates, and, as late as 1814, 96,000 people paid a penny to stare at the antics within its walls. The word 'bedlam', a corrupted form of Bethlehem, entered our language from this source.

That 15th century Ottoman hospital was not an isolated aberration. The so-called 'Golden Age' of Islamic culture, from the 9th to the 13th century, produced the world's first hospitals, and the world's oldest degree-granting university. The concept of 'doctorate' originated in their teaching of law and the issuing of licenses to practise. İbn al Hasan (Latinised as Alhacen or Alhazen) is credited with being the world's first true scientist. I haven't seen it myself, but I have it on good authority that you can see, in a chamber of the US House of Representatives, a likeness of the 16th century Ottoman Sultan Suleiman, in recognition of his codification of an entire system of jurisprudence.

Well, from such heights, how can I descend to the bathetic depths of baklava, Turkish Delight and sherbet; of sofas and divans; of kiosks, bazaars, lutes and Turkish carpets; of syrups, elixirs and genies? I don't intend to even mention the Turkish bath. It seems unlikely that those Asian invaders brought them brick by brick on horseback from the steppes. Simply, I would like to leave you with two verses from the Rubaiyat of the 11th century Persian poet, Omar Khayyam:

But leave the wise to wrangle, and with me,
The quarrel of the universe let be,
And in some corner of the hubbub couched,
Make game of that which makes as much of thee.

There, with a loaf of bread, beneath the bough,
A flask of wine, a book of verse, and thou
Beside me, singing in the wilderness,
And wilderness is paradise enow[16].

---

[16] I think he wanted to say 'enough', but it didn't rhyme!

21

Merry Sufi Christmas and a Happy Chinese New Year!

8 January 2011

First up, I want to wish all my loyal readers (and any new-comers to the fold) health, happiness and prosperity in the New Year, the Year of Our Lord, 2011. Uh oh, just a moment – let me adjust that – 2011 CE[17]. It was a measure of the grip globalisation has on us all, that midnight, December 31st was celebrated with parties and festivities from Sydney to Seoul; from Auckland to Amritsar and Allahabad; in Times Square, New York, and Times Square, Hong Kong; that the world's most expensive Christmas tree was to be found in Abu Dhabi, and the tallest New Year fireworks display, in Dubai, on the 828 metre Burj Khalifa. Even the Chinese joined the party, despite the fact that their new year, the Year of the Rabbit, incidentally, and 4707, 4708, or 4647, depending on who's counting, will not click over until February 3rd.

I kind of liked that. I've never been a big capitalist, but you have to respect the power of an idea to bring people together, don't you! Socialism has been dead and buried for a few years now, and life is getting increasingly difficult for religious fanatics. But Mammon is hard at

---

[17] Common Era

work out there, binding Hindus, Buddhists, Christians, Muslims, atheists and reformed Communists into one big happy family. It's pretty clear that there's never been an '–ism' like Capitalism!

However, in the midst of all the Santa Clauses, Father Christmases, New Year pyrotechnics and what not, another date slipped by pretty much unnoticed . . . the 17th of December. I hope the Sufis among you will forgive my stating the obvious, but that day marked the 737th anniversary of the death of Mevlana Jalal al-din Rumi, the 13th century Persian poet, jurist, theologian, philosopher and Sufi mystic, known in the West more simply as Rumi. I have to admit, though, I might have missed the date too, if one of my students hadn't pointed it out to me. Nevertheless, once it was drawn to my attention, it got me thinking . . .

Those of you who have read this far will know how much I love my adoptive home, the Republic of Turkey, and the respect I have for my Muslim brothers and sisters who have become my friends, neighbours and even family. You will perhaps have marvelled that the son of a nation that once joined a military invasion to subdue this land, could have stayed so long, and developed such affection for former enemies. But there it is, and I make no apologies.

Still, if there is one thing I can't get my head around, it's the lunar calendar. I'm a firm believer in a fair day's work for a fair day's pay – but I like holidays, nonetheless. I'm used to my Christmases and Easters and New Years and Labour Days and Queen's Birthdays, and all that stuff we take as an inalienable human right back in New Zealand. I may have seemed to take it for granted when I was younger, but I have always been grateful to those nameless activists who fought to ensure that, even though no one was exactly sure when Jesus was nailed to that tree, we would get a Friday and a Monday off school or work every year in sympathy. No doubt those in the know always got together on the correct day to cheer Elizabeth Regina as she blew out her birthday candles – but we in New Zealand could always count on the first Monday in June as the day for honouring our sovereign lady queen.

It therefore seems to me that no one would suffer much harm, and the devout could continue to sacrifice and fast, if the Muslim holy times of Ramadan and Eid al-Adha (Kurban Bayram) were similarly fixed, perhaps sometime in autumn and spring. I understand that, for tribes living in a harsh desert environment not much conducive to sowing and harvesting, solar seasons were pretty irrelevant, and the phases of the moon seemed as good a measure of the passing of time as any other. If you can sleep through the heat of a desert day, fasting from dawn till dusk may not be such a trial. If you're not bound to the five-day working week, it may not matter much if your days of feasting fall on weekends or weekdays. But these days, when we are all, to a greater or lesser extent in the clutches of the above-mentioned Mammon, it makes a big difference. We need to feel that we can plan our lives (including our holidays) and that important festivals will take place at stable and predictable times each year - and, for better or worse, that means the solar year.

Sure, I know what you're thinking. Those Islamic months are set in stone. God gave the Koran to the Angel Gabriel, who gave it to the Prophet Mohammed, and that's it, end of story. No amendments, no interpretations, no alterations. Lunar months are ordained by God. The Ramazan month of fasting will start when the '*Hilal*' crescent at the beginning of the ninth lunar month is spotted by the official 'spotter'. Any government of a Muslim country that tried to 'rationalise' the calendar for the modern world would be committing political suicide. But spare a thought for the poor school kids, who will soon face an academic year without a break because the religious holidays all fall during the summer vacation. What of the employed faithful who will have to work through 28 summer days without letting a sip of water pass their lips? Anyway, with Muslims spread all over the globe, there's no way that one 'spotter' can do the job for the whole community any more.

And there's another thing – the reason I brought up Mevlana Rumi in the first place, in case you were wondering. Did you notice that date, 17 December 1273? And did you wonder, as I did, why it wasn't 6 Jumada al-Thani, 672 A.H[18]? Well, again, I have to admit, I found a site on the Internet[19] to do the conversion for me, but you get the point I want to make. There was a guy who was born, lived and died a Muslim in important cities in an Islamic empire at a time when that religion was assuredly in the ascendant. Thousands of devout Muslims visit his tomb in the Turkish city of Konya every year. Without doubt, the date on his tombstone would read (if we could read Arabic) 672, and not 1273. Yet every year, around 17 December, a clearly non-lunar date, Muslim Turks

---

[18] 'After Hijrah' – the year according to the Muslim calendar.

[19] http://www.islamicfinder.org/dateConversion.php

welcome the faithful and the interested, to join them in commemorating the passing on of the great Sufi mystic.

Well, I don't know about you, but I'm glad to find there is one other '–ism' with an interest in bringing folks together, rather than tearing them apart. I don't want to get into the debate about whether Islam is a religion of war or peace. It seems to me that, depending on where you're starting from, you could argue either way, just as you could for most other religions and ideologies.

Mevlana Rumi, however, was '. . . *not a Muslim of the orthodox type. His doctrine advocates unlimited tolerance, positive reasoning, goodness, charity and awareness through love. To him and to his disciples all religions are more or less truth. Looking with the same eye on Muslim, Jew and Christian alike, his peaceful and tolerant teaching has appealed to* [people] *of all sects and creeds.'* [20]

The United Nations Educational, Scientific and Cultural Organisation (UNESCO) organised events to commemorate, in 2007, the 800th anniversary of the birth of Mevlana Rumi. They did this because they believed that his ideas and ideals coincided with the ideals of UNESCO, which you can find on their website[21]:

'UNESCO *works to create the conditions for dialogue among civilizations, cultures and peoples, based upon respect for commonly shared values. It is through this dialogue that the world can achieve global visions of sustainable development encompassing observance of human rights, mutual respect and the alleviation of poverty, all of which are at the heart of UNESCO's mission and activities.*

'UNESCO's *mission is to contribute to the building of peace, the eradication of poverty, sustainable development and intercultural dialogue through education, the sciences, culture, communication and information.*'

Pretty good stuff, you have to admit. And if Rumi believed in that, then I'm with him, even if he was a Muslim.

[20] www.mevlana.net/

[21] UNESCO website: http://www.unesco.org/new/en/unesco/about-us/who-we-are/introducing-unesco/

22

Turkey and the European Union

13 January 2011

OK – A geography question for all you pub trivia freaks out there. What's the capital city of Estonia? Yeah, I know it's on the tip of your tongue. Come on, spit it out! Tallinn, right? Bravo, well, done! And, of course, you knew it was European Capital of Culture in 2011, right? Along with Turku, Finland? Seems the gnomes of Brussels accept that they erred in 2010. Essen, Pecs and Istanbul were just too many culture capitals for one year; so from now on, they've decided two at a time will be enough.

So, it looks as though we have two things to congratulate the Estonians on. The other, of course, is their elevation to membership of the EU Euro club as of 1 January 2011. No doubt the Germans will be delighted to know they've got the 'Baltic Tiger' at their side to help bail out those frailer members of the club: Greece, Ireland, and the other ones making up the economic barnyard of 'PIIGS'.

But seriously, folks, I really have to admit I knew nothing about Estonia until I read that news item on the latest member of the Euro Club ... so I checked them out, and I want to share my findings with you.

I had previously heard of the 'Baltic Tiger' – apparently a reference to their booming economy around the time they were accepted into the EU in 2004. Sadly, it seems the growl has gone out of the beast in recent times. The CIA World Factbook website[22] reports that, since the real estate bubble burst in 2008, their economy has been contracting at an annual rate of around 15 percent, one of the highest (or lowest) rates in the world.

Still, the Germans don't need to fear a major drain on their financial largesse. According to the 2000 census, Estonia had a total population of 1,370,000 – not a figure to strike fear into anyone's heart. Interestingly, according to latest estimates, that population has fallen by 30,000 in ten years. Wonder where they went?

Another item of interest I came across on the CIA site, and I'm quoting here:

Estonia is *a 'growing producer of synthetic drugs; increasingly important transhipment zone for cannabis, cocaine, opiates, and synthetic drugs since joining the European Union and the Schengen Accord;* [there is] *potential money laundering related to organized crime and drug trafficking is a concern, as is possible use of the gambling sector to launder funds; major use of opiates and ecstasy.'*

Well, that's enough on Estonia. I don't want to dwell on their plight – looks like they've got enough troubles to go on with. However, the news about their joining the Euro club did prompt me to check out one or two other recent additions to the united Europe. Bulgaria and Romania were judged to have met the EU's membership conditions, and joined on 1 January 2007. *BBC News*, around that time, ran an article on the subject, asking, among other questions, whether these two former Communist countries were really ready for membership. Again, I'm quoting:

'*Officials at the European Commission* [were] *quoted as saying that they are not really ready, but that delaying accession may not be the best way to encourage further reforms. The Commission was hoping, for example,*

---

[22] https://www.cia.gov/library/publications/the-world-factbook/geos/en.html

that Bulgaria would take big steps over the summer to tackle high-level corruption and organized crime, but officials in Brussels say they have been disappointed.'[23]

According to the same report, Albania, Bosnia, Kosovo, Montenegro and Serbia are expected to join in the near future. Meanwhile, Turkey's membership talks are on again-off again, which brings me to the point of this chapter. I've just been reading an interview[24] with a Turkish academic, Dr Armağan Emre Çakır, assistant professor at the European Union Institute of Marmara University in Istanbul. Dr Çakır has, I understand, recently published a book entitled 'Fifty Years of EU-Turkey Relations: A Sisyphean Story'.

Now Sisyphus, as I'm sure you are aware, was a king in ancient times who was punished by the gods in a particularly infuriating way. A thoroughly objectionable character, Sisyphus apparently let it be known that he considered himself superior, not only to his mortal subjects, but to the gods themselves. His divine punishment was to roll, for all eternity, a huge boulder to the top of a hill. The fiendish nature of the punishment was that, with the summit in sight, the boulder would roll back down to the bottom, whence the unfortunate king would have to begin his task again.

Now, I haven't read Dr Çakır's book, so I can't say whether, with this analogy, he is comparing Turkey to the obnoxious King Sisyphus, justly punished; or Turkey's attempts to join the EU to the task of rolling the boulder uphill. In the interview, the learned professor claimed that he had taken great pains to avoid seeming biased in Turkey's favour, so it may, indeed, be the former.

Nevertheless, I checked out the other part of the title, and it's true: Turkey did, in fact, first apply to what was then the EEC (European Economic Community) for associate membership in July 1958. Almost 30 years later, in April 1987, after making little appreciable progress, the Turks applied for formal membership into what was now the European Community. Since then, the occasional crumb has been thrown their

---

[23] http://news.bbc.co.uk/2/hi/europe/2266385.stm

[24] http://changingturkey.com/2011/01/08/interview-with-dr-armagan-emre-cakir-on-turkey-eu-relations/

way. In 1995, for example, a customs union agreement was signed between the EU and Turkey. One assumes, the thinking behind this is to
keep them nibbling at the hook – to keep them believing that acceptance is just around the corner, if they'll only try a little harder.

You can understand why Europe would want to do that. Turkey has
been a member of NATO since its inception, and has always been a major contributor to its military forces. The US maintains at least one air
force base on the Turkish mainland, and makes it clear to all and sundry
that Turkey is an important 'friend'. Turkey joined the Council of Europe
in 1949 and the OSCE (Organisation for Security and Cooperation in
Europe) in 1973. Coming straight out and telling them to get lost is
clearly out of the question.

On the other hand, to accede to the EU, Turkey must first success-
fully complete negotiations with the European Commission on each
of the 35 chapters of the *acquis communautaire*, the total body of EU
law. Afterwards, the member states must unanimously agree on granting
Turkey membership to the European Union. And the day that happens,
a squadron of flying pigs will land at Istanbul International Airport, and
be given an official welcome.

Call me a cynic, but I can't see either event happening. Whatever
misgivings Europe has about Turkey's political and social fabric, it is
clear that, when they want to accept a country into their fold, they do
so, in the stated belief that desirable change is more likely to take place
once that country has become a member. One of the major sticking
points in Turkey's on-going negotiations for membership is the Cyprus
situation. In 2004, the Secretary-General of the United Nations, Kofi
Annan, submitted a plan for the reunification of the island. The plan
was supported by Turkey and the Turkish Cypriots, but rejected by the
Greeks. Shortly thereafter, the (Greek) Republic of (Southern)[25] Cyprus
was admitted to membership of the EU.

I can't escape the feeling that the antics of Western leaders re Turkey's
application for EU membership are simply a variation of the 'good cop-
bad cop' routine. The UK Prime Minister and the US President, and
the occasional other high profile politico, regularly go public with state-
ments about the desirability of admitting Turkey. However, for my mon-

---

[25] My parentheses, of course.

ey, I'd give more credence to the words of French President Sarkozy, and German Chancellor Merkel, both of whom have made it abundantly clear that they see no place for Turkey in the European Union.

Would it be surprising, then, if Turkey began to take an increasingly independent stance on international affairs; and to seek economic and strategic alliances elsewhere?

23

Who Killed the Armenians?

13 February 2011

There is currently a resolution before the United States Congress to give official recognition to the event in 1915 often referred to as 'The Armenian Genocide', and to incorporate this recognition into US foreign policy. For the sake of brevity, this resolution is referred to as *H.Res.252*, and it was introduced in March 2009. Barack Obama, prior to his election as President, made it clear that he fully supported such official recognition. It is a measure, then, of the controversial nature of the issue that, two years on, the resolution has not been passed, and very likely never will be. Mr Obama, for his part, seems to have cooled on the issue.

I doubt that any of my readers are ignorant of the claims underlying this resolution, but, to be fair, let's hear them from the Armenian National Institute:

'The Armenian Genocide was centrally planned and administered by the Turkish government against the entire Armenian population of the Ottoman Empire. It was carried out during W.W.I between the years

1915 and 1918. The Armenian people were subjected to deportation, expropriation, abduction, torture, massacre, and starvation. The great bulk of the Armenian population was forcibly removed from Armenia and Anatolia to Syria, where the vast majority was sent into the desert to die of thirst and hunger. Large numbers of Armenians were methodically massacred throughout the Ottoman Empire. Women and children were abducted and horribly abused. The entire wealth of the Armenian people was expropriated. After only a little more than a year of calm at the end of W.W.I, the atrocities were renewed between 1920 and 1923, and the remaining Armenians were subjected to further massacres and expulsions ... It is estimated that one and a half million Armenians perished between 1915 and 1923.' [26]*

Sounds bad, for sure, and not something that can be easily dismissed. However, no event in history can be isolated from what preceded it, so I plan to take you on a trip back in time. Before departure, though, I want to draw your attention to a small but significant detail in the first sentence of the ANI statement above: '*the genocide was planned and administered by the <u>Turkish</u> government between the years of 1915-1918*'. Admittedly there is a reference, later in the same sentence, to the Ottoman Empire, but I am sure the distortion is deliberate. In fact, there was no Turkish Government until it was established when the Republic of Turkey came into being in 1923, just as there was no United States Government until independence from Britain was declared in 1776.

I am not, at this stage, taking issue with anything else in the ANI's statement – merely clearing the way for our journey back to an earlier and arguably happier time in the Ottoman Empire, whose government should more correctly stand accused. Generally dated from 1299, it was one of the longer-lasting empires in world history, and one of its features, little-known but deserving of recognition, was the 'millet' system of administration. A 'millet' was a community of faith whose members formed a relatively autonomous group within the empire. They had their own leader, administered their own laws at a local level, collected and disbursed taxes, practised their own religion, educated their children, spoke their own language – and lived alongside members of the other millets in comparative harmony.

---

[26] Armenian National Institute: http://www.armenian-genocide.org/

There were five millets in the Ottoman Empire: Muslims (not just Turks, by the way), Orthodox Christians, Armenian Christians, Jews, and later, Syriac Orthodox Christians. It was a system based on religion rather than race or nationality, because that's the way the world was in those days. No doubt as a system of government it had its imperfections, but set it alongside what existed in Europe at the same time and it looks like a beacon of tolerance and open-mindedness. Take Spain, for example, as Roman Catholicism established itself in the Iberian Peninsula to the accompaniment of Inquisitorial torture, burnings and forced conversions of Muslims and Jews. Many of those Jews accepted the invitation of Sultan Beyazit to settle in the Ottoman Empire, and their descendants can be found in Istanbul today, worshipping in their medieval Spanish dialect[27].

So maybe the question arises in your mind, as it did in mine: if the Ottomans were so tolerant and open-minded, why did they suddenly decide to commit genocide on those poor, harmless, law-abiding Armenians? The roots of the answer lie in the growth of the major European powers during the 18th century, the ideas of the Enlightenment and the associated forces of Romantic Nationalism and Imperialism. The Ottomans had been a (if not the) major European power until the end of the 17th century, but times were a-changing. In particular, the imperial ambitions of its northern neighbour, Russia, were threatening its territorial integrity. Russia was expanding in all directions, but its southern march posed the greatest threat to the Ottomans. As they moved towards the Black Sea, into the Crimea and the Caucasus, the Russians pursued a policy of Russification, killing and displacing the majority Muslim inhabitants of those lands and replacing them with Christian Russians, Slavs and if necessary, Armenians.

As well as loss of territory, another negative result of this for the Ottomans was an enormous influx of penniless refugees who had to be fed, housed and settled – a huge financial drain on an empire that was already struggling economically. The Russian advance into Ottoman territory continued right into the First World War, and the Armenian population became an increasingly important tool in their expansion. It suited the Russian cause to encourage Armenian nationalism with promises of support for the creation of an independent state in return

---

[27] http://en.wikipedia.org/wiki/Sephardi_Jews

for assistance against their Ottoman overlords. The Ottoman government and its Muslim subjects, for their part, became increasingly intolerant of Armenian acts of insurrection and terrorism within their borders. It is interesting to note that, when the Ottoman Empire finally collapsed at the end of the Great War, far from supporting their independence, the new Communist Government of Russia swallowed the Armenians into their Soviet maw in 1921, after a scant three years of national sovereignty.

However, I'm getting ahead of myself here. There was one positive outcome for the Ottomans, at least in the short term, from the emergence of the Russian threat. The other European powers, in particular Britain and France, began to take an interest in the unfolding events. For a start, they were determined to prevent the Russians from achieving their ambition of controlling the Istanbul straits and gaining free access to the warm waters of the Mediterranean. One of the key issues in the foreign policy of all the European powers in the 19th century was what became known as 'The Eastern Question', the essence of which was: *When will the ailing Ottoman Empire finally collapse, and which of us will get what parts of it when it does?* The corollary of wanting to get the best bits for yourself, of course, was, naturally, ensuring that your rivals didn't get them.

In practice, this policy involved encouraging national consciousness among the subject peoples of the Ottoman Empire in order to hasten its fragmentation and demise. Needless to say, it is not to be thought that the European powers concerned had any great love of nationalism as a philosophy *per se*. If you have any doubts about this, ask the Irish or the Indians, or the Algerians, or the Turkic peoples of Central Asia. The first 'nation' to benefit, however, was the Greeks, the success of whose struggle for independence was ensured by the intervention of the British, French and Russian navies, which combined to destroy the Ottoman fleet in 1827. A little publicized side effect of Greek independence was the massacre and/or displacement of thousands of Muslims whose families had lived there for centuries.

The original Greek state established at this time was perhaps only forty percent of its present area. Over the next century, successive governments took advantage of the weakening and embattled Ottomans to expand their domains northwards and eastwards into Macedonia, the

Balkans and the Aegean Islands. As they advanced, non-Christian minorities were slaughtered or driven out. An interesting example is the city of Salonika, which fell to the Greeks in 1912. At that time the second city of the Ottoman Empire, Selanik had the largest Jewish population of any city in Europe. Fifty percent of its inhabitants were Jewish, twenty-five percent Muslim and the remainder, mostly Orthodox Christian. In 1917, a mysterious fire broke out destroying most of the Jewish and Muslim parts of town. Subsequently most of the Jews and Muslims, prevented from rebuilding their homes and businesses, departed. There were still, however, a large number of Jews in Salonika when Nazi Germany invaded in 1941. As far as I know, there is no suggestion that the Greeks conspired with the Nazis to exterminate the Jews – but they certainly benefited from the destruction of the large historic Jewish cemetery, where the city's university is now located.

Interestingly, if you visit Istanbul and make inquiries, you will be shown numerous Greek Orthodox, Armenian and Jewish churches, synagogues and cemeteries occupying large and prominent sites in very pleasant parts of the city. The land they stand on must be almost priceless – yet they remain, respected and untouched in this nation of Muslims. In contrast, Athens is one of the few European capital cities that lacks a functioning mosque, despite the existence of half a million Muslim residents[28].

Which brings me back to the Armenians – whom I am sure you were beginning to think I had forgotten. I mentioned, above, that the Russian Empire massacred and expelled hundreds of thousands of Muslims (Tatars, Circassians and Abhazis) as it expanded into the Crimea from the 1770s, and the Caucasus from the 1790s[29]. An article in a recent *Time* magazine[30] discussing the January 2011 terrorist attack at the Moscow airport, alleged a link to Chechen activists, and blamed the situation on two hundred years of Russian oppression. As occupied territories were cleared of their Muslim inhabitants, they were systematically resettled with Christians, more likely to be supportive of their co-religionist overlords. Among the groups used as pawns in this game of Russification were the Armenians, many of whom were invited to

---

[28] http://www.nytimes.com/2007/07/05/world/europe/05iht-greek.1.6505511.html

[29] http://everything2.com/title/Russian+Expansion+in+the+19th+Century

[30] *Putin's Terrorist Problem*, Time European Edition, February 7, 2011

occupy the homes and farms of the dispossessed Muslims (expropriation seems to have been a common enough occurrence in those days).
Undoubtedly the Muslim refugees who flooded into Ottoman Anatolia
would have harboured some resentment against the people who were
seen to be profiting from their tragedy, and we need look no further for
the roots of the sectarian hatred that began to build through the 19th
century.

As an interesting aside[31], there are attempts internationally to have
present-day Russia acknowledge a 'Circassian Genocide' that allegedly
took place in the second half of the 19th century. The Putin government,
not unreasonably, rejects responsibility for events that took place under
the Czarist regime – yet, according to the *Time* article cited above, similar policies continue to be implemented against Muslims in the area to
this day.

What happened in Anatolia during the 19th century, then, was increasing encroachment on Ottoman territory by the Russians, and
increasing desperation in the Ottoman Empire as their boundaries re-
treated, impoverished refugees flooded in with tales of horror, and members of the Armenian 'millet' (see above), encouraged by the Russians,
increasingly resorted to terrorist attacks and insurgency.

But let's not pick on Russia alone. I recently came across writings
of a gentleman by the name of Edward J Erickson[32]. Apparently he is
a retired regular US Army officer at the Marine Corps University in
Virginia, recognized as an authority on the Ottoman Army during the
First World War. He writes of the activities of the Royal Navy in the
Eastern Mediterranean from December 1914. In particular he refers to
an RN cruiser, HMS *Doris*, commanded by a Captain Frank Larkin,
which conducted operations around the Ottoman port of Iskenderun
(Alexandretta), shelling shore installations and gathering intelligence
from local Armenians. Erickson suggests that the Ottoman high com-
mand expected an allied invasion. They did not know where it would
take place (with hindsight, we know it was directed at Gallipoli and
the Dardanelles), but the rail links near Iskenderun were of enormous
strategic importance to the Ottoman forces, and at the same time, very

[31] 'The Circassian Genocide': http://www.circassian-genocide.info/

[32] 'Turkish Coalition of America': http://www.tc-america.org/media/Ericson_Larki-
nandtheTurks.pdf

vulnerable to a sea-launched attack. Erickson suggests that the activities of Captain Larkin and the *Doris*, as well as the military incursions and machinations of the Russians, were instrumental in the decision to 'relocate' Armenians later in 1915.

In fact, 'relocate' is Dr Erickson's word, not mine. Undoubtedly, Armenian people in the east of Anatolia suffered a terrible tragedy. I do not have the space here to discuss the extent to which the present Republic of Turkey should be held responsible for the sins of the Ottoman Empire; nor whether there was actually an official government decision, and if so, what its aims were. I do not intend to get involved in the discussion of how many Armenians died (also, apparently, a highly debatable issue), nor to question why so many Armenians remained in Istanbul, the seat of Ottoman Government, retaining their property, churches and cemeteries to the present day. My aim has been solely to suggest that whatever happened in that part of the world in 1915 needs to be seen in terms of events leading up to it in the previous 130 years[33]. To compare what happened with the Armenians of the Ottoman Empire to the Nazi German extermination of the Jewish people is not only a distortion of historical evidence, but a grave injustice to the victims of the Nazi holocaust.

---

[33] Check, for example, 'The Forgotten Minorities of Eastern Europe', Ed. Arno Tanner

24

New Zealand and Turkey - What's the Connection?

24 March 2011

Countries located on geological fault lines have been getting a hard time recently. Two events in particular hit home to me. First there was the 6.3 quake that devastated New Zealand's second-largest city, Christchurch. More recently, a tsunami generated by an 8.9 seismic monster levelled coastal towns and cities in Japan.

I was watching and reading about the tragic events from my home in Istanbul, and I was struck once again by the kindness and concern of my Turkish friends and neighbours. People here were constantly approaching me and asking about events back 'home' - was my family ok? Luckily, they are, but another thing to strike me was how large a part luck, or fate, plays in these tragedies.

Didem Yaman was a young woman from Çanakkale in Turkey – ironically the town on the Dardanelles that Turks associate with the campaign known to New Zealanders as Gallipoli. Unfortunately there is more than one irony here. Didem was interested in the Asia Pacific region and her English was so good that she was accepted by Otago University to study for a doctorate in International Relations. Her area of interest was historical ties between Turkey and Australia and New

Zealand. She had been in NZ for four years, living in Dunedin, but she made the ill-fated trip up to Christchurch to visit a friend – a Chinese friend in fact, from a country also known for its earthquakes. Didem's family continued to hope that their daughter was alive, despite not having heard from her since the earthquake – until (irony upon irony) her body was discovered in the ruins of a health clinic, located in a collapsed shopping centre.

The main reason why Turks are so sympathetic towards people affected by earthquakes is, I guess, that Turkey itself sits astride several major fault lines, and has experienced its share of seismic disasters over the years. One of the most recent was the Marmara event that left at least 17,000 dead on 17 August 1999. I wasn't in Turkey at the time, but I remember it well because I missed it by one day. On 11 August there was a solar eclipse, and I was drying out on the beach after a swim in Lake Van as it began. I was out in the east of Turkey visiting places a little off the normal tourist track, and I donned my special spectacles to watch the moon move slowly across the face of the sun – not quite 100 percent blackout, but maybe 95 percent, and quite impressive. Less than a week later I flew to London, and woke up on the morning of 18 August to read about the 7.6 magnitude quake that had followed the eclipse and caused so much damage and loss of life.

The town in Turkey, where Didem Yaman's family mourned the loss of their daughter, is, of course, the focus of a minor migration from Australia and New Zealand every year. It is the most convenient base from which to visit the beaches, ravines and ridges that were the stage for the horrific slaughter of young men in 1915 that Turks call the Battle of Çanakkale.

On 25 April, thousands of mostly young Australians and New Zealanders gather at dawn on the other side of the narrow strait that witnessed the spilling of so much blood and the loss of so many young lives. The day has assumed an importance in both countries out of proportion to its significance as a historical event. The eight-month campaign, which can only really be viewed as a sideshow to the main events of the Great War, and a wasteful defeat that prolonged the bloodbath in the trenches of the Western Front, has taken on a powerful symbolism for antipodeans. Two small nations, whose constitutions still recognise the Queen of England as head of state, have come to see Anzac

Day as the defining moment in their search for an independent identity. Lacking an Independence Day, or a Republic Day, and with some misgivings about the traditional days inherited from their origins as outposts of empire, New Zealanders and Australians have adopted the day of the Gallipoli landings as marking the beginnings of the emergence of a national consciousness.

I say 'the beginnings of the emergence', because clearly the participants at the time were not suddenly struck with a 'Road to Damascus' experience. It has been a slow, developmental process, but undoubtedly the experience of the ANZACs was pivotal. For a start there was the journey. Although the first convoy set out from Albany in Western Australia, and, passing through the Suez Canal, went only as far as Alexandria in Egypt, the sea voyage, with the benefit of steam engines, took a month. Perhaps it crossed the minds of those young men that their great grandfathers and grandmothers, 75 years earlier, had spent four months on a sailing ship to make the journey in reverse. They must have begun to realise how far removed in space they now were from the land of their ancestors.

And now they found themselves on an alien shore, served up as cannon fodder to a foe against whom they had no grievance, by officers and politicians whose aims and motives had no relevance to their own lives and experience. The survivors who made it back to their southern hemisphere homes were lauded as heroes for defending an empire they had mostly ceased to believe in – and their experiences laid the foundation for the sense of selfhood and nationhood that slowly began to emerge over the next half century or so. The distance from Europe had become spiritual as much as spatial.

In terms of written history, New Zealand and Australia are suckling babes compared to the lands that make up modern Turkey. Here rise the two rivers that bound Mesopotamia, one of the original birthplaces of civilisation. Here can be found the mountain on which Noah's Ark is said to have grounded as the floodwaters of the deluge receded. So many more biblical events recorded in the Old and New Testaments took place here; so much of what we think of as Greek or Roman history and mythology unfolded here. The annals of history stretch back so far that the Turks, who have been here for a thousand years and more, are still looked on by some as newcomers and interlopers.

Therein lies another connection I want to make between Turkey and New Zealand. Here are the Turks, on the back doorstep of Europe, speaking a language few outsiders can understand, with their roots way out in Central Asia. Show them, however, a TV channel from just across the border in Azerbaijan and most of them experience mild culture shock. As for their Turkic cousins in Kazakhstan, Kirghizstan or Tuva, they may feel some distant twinges of kinship, but there is no going back. Whatever Europeans may think, Turkey is not Asia. Its European credentials go back to Alexander the Great and beyond. For the same reason, whatever Turkish nationalists may wish to believe, the modern Turk has little or no genetic connection to the warrior horsemen that swept out of Central Asia in Europe's darkest ages.

In much the same way, New Zealanders find themselves well settled on an island group in the South Pacific Ocean – speaking English in a region where Austronesian and Asiatic languages are the norm. Our cultural roots are half a world away, in the British Isles – but when we go there for our customary OE, or to research a family tree, we quickly realise that 'we' are not 'they', and 'they' are not 'we'. For New Zealanders and Turks, the questions 'Who are we?' and 'Why are we here?' have more significance than mere philosophical pondering.

I want to return now briefly to that normally sleepy town on the Dardanelles. Unlike New Zealand and Australia, Turkey is a republic. Its head of state is a president elected by its own parliament. The people have their own Republic Day (29 October) on which to unite in pyrotechnic celebrations. The town of Çanakkale, however, awakes each year from its customary drowsiness on 18 March, and it can be argued that this date has more significance to the existence of modern Turkey. I have discussed elsewhere why the Turks celebrate their victory on that date, while we allies of the British prefer to think that we weren't defeated until our final evacuation from the Gallipoli Peninsula eight months later. Be that as it may, the crucial point for Turkey is that the Battle of Çanakkale represented their one outstanding victory in an otherwise bleak war. The architect and inspiration of the success was Colonel Mustafa Kemal who went on to lead the army of national independence and become the first president of the Republic of Turkey. Most foreign visitors are puzzled and a little incredulous at the manifest signs of adulation directed towards Atatürk – but to Turks, he is the *sine qua non* of their existence as a nation. Turning back the invasion at Gallipoli undoubtedly earned him the credibility that powered him to his later achievements.

New Zealand is a small country with a tiny population, far from the halls, corridors and stages of geopolitical events – unlike Turkey, which is right there, on the spot and un-ignorable. For decades, Turkey was one of the major bulwarks of NATO and Europe when the former Soviet Union was vying with the USA for world domination. Hard to imagine now, but so it was, until the Soviet Russian Empire began to disintegrate in 1989. Most of us didn't know it at the time, when the late great President Kennedy was self-righteously ordering the Soviets to remove their missiles from Cuba – but he and his Pentagon buddies had several bases in Turkey with their own nuclear hardware trained on the Russkies. For sure, the Russians knew, though, and had Turkey high on their list of targets for pre-emptive or retaliatory strikes. Even today, the US maintains a military base in the South East of Turkey, and George Bush Snr was happy to use it in launching his Operation Desert Storm. Western Europe has good reasons to be grateful to Turkey – yet it is unlikely they will ever welcome their big, loyal eastern cousin into their EU club. Well, these days you might think that acceptance would be a mixed blessing anyway, but still . . .

New Zealand, on the other hand, has never been of strategic importance in anyone's plans for world domination – and thank God for that, say I! But we have played our part over the years, following, first Mother England, and later Uncle Sam, into wars which were of very peripheral concern to us: the Boer War, the First and Second World Wars, Korea, Viet Nam . . . We even made one or two offers that weren't taken up. But when we tried to get involved in the big boys' games, like asking the French to please explode their experimental nuclear bombs a little closer to their own backyard, did we get any support? A gang of French 'secret' agents bombed a *Greenpeace* protest vessel right in the centre of our largest city. Luckily, they were so incompetent that our police caught them – but then our government was forced to bow to diplomatic pressure and let the buggers go. Thanks, friends!

Well, sometimes I get tired of international politics, and I'm sure you do too, so let's go back into history, where I, for one, feel a lot more comfortable. There's a fair dollop of Scottish blood in my family tree, as there is in that of many New Zealanders. Even today, some of us are not averse to donning a kilt, if we've got the legs for it, skirling the pipes, or sipping a wee dram at Hogmanay. Scottish history is a complex business for such a small country, not helped by the likes of Mel Gibson confusing issues here, and oversimplifying them there. However, most of us like to feel a certain kinship with those mad Gaelic highlanders who needed a wall to keep them from rustling the Sassenach's cattle.

Imagine my surprise, nay, disbelief, when, on a journey into the remote mountains of Turkey's Black Sea coast, I followed a strange melodious wailing in the village I was visiting, and came upon a young man playing . . . a bagpipe! Sure enough! They call it *tulum* in those parts, and it's a more primitive instrument, lacking the drones of its Scottish relative – but a relative nonetheless. No one really seems to know where those Celts and Gaels came from, though some suggest a Circassian or Central Asian origin. From there they spread all over Europe and, yes, Anatolia. Their name is immortalised in the name of the comic strip hero, Asterix the Gaul, and in the country Wales, which Turks, interestingly, call '*Galler*'. The New Testament evangelist Paul, renowned for his epistles, wrote one to the Galatians, inhabitants of the region around modern Ankara, whose name again preserves their Gaelic heritage. Even in Istanbul itself, the area beside the Golden Horn, where Europeans set up their trade and diplomatic posts, is known as Galata, and some say this name has its origins in those early Scottish ancestors!

I want to conclude this discussion of the similarities between Turkey and New Zealand with a nod in the direction of my hippy flower power youth, and a return to nature. Everyone in the world surely knows that New Zealand is the cleanest, greenest country on earth, even if we ourselves know that we are continually doing our best to screw up the beauty God gave us. We are proud that our country was the most authentic place to shoot the 'Lord of the Rings' movies. Most of us appreciate the chance we still have to tramp through primeval forests and dive into crystal clear pools beneath pristine cascades of snow melt rivers flowing from majestic alpine peaks. We identify strongly with our flightless avian symbol, the *kiwi*, and take pride in the fact that this word from the language of our indigenous Maori race has found its way into most languages of the civilised world. We are less proud of the fact that 277 species of our native flora and fauna are listed as endangered, but we care, we really do.

Everyone in the world may be less aware that Turkey has 167 species on that same list – nothing much to be proud of, until you consider that, at least those species still exist in Turkey, when they have been pretty much wiped out from the rest of Europe and the Middle East. The closest thing I have seen to the forests of West Coast New Zealand is the Black Sea region of Turkey, where a snow-capped 4000 metre mountain range plunges down through rain-forested slopes to the coast, sending fast-flowing rivers through precipitous gorges to the sea. Turkey has huge biogeographical diversity, and is a key location for many species of migratory birds. The largest remaining stands of Lebanese cedar are here, as well as breeding places for the Mediterranean monk seal and the caretta caretta turtle. Contrary to popularly spread rumours, the first episode of 'Star Wars' was not filmed in Cappadocia, but it might have been, if George Lucas had got his way – in which case, it could well have been an even more spectacular film.

I confess, there are times when I feel a long way from home – and, measured in kilometres, it's a major trip, for sure. But most of the time I feel remarkably at home in Turkey, largely because the people are hospitable, just like us.

25

Islamic Dominoes - Will the populist uprisings spread to Turkey?

15 April 2011

It looks like a crusading Republican president's ultimate fantasy come true! Populist uprisings sweeping fundamentalist dictators from power throughout the Islamic world, bringing democracy to the oppressed and opening new markets for *Coca Cola* and *Subway*. Pity it had to happen while a Democrat was in the White House; and pity for the Democrats that it had to be their man who launched the next military strike on an asymmetrical foe. Nevertheless, when things at home are not looking so rosy, it's a positive sign for the American Way that its greatest perceived threat is seen to be succumbing to the rising power of democracy from within.

Unfortunately, global events are rarely so simple. The reality on the ground is rather more complex. I want to take a quick look at what seems to be happening in Muslim lands in the Middle East and around the Mediterranean from the point of view of one living in such a land. First of all, then, a brief round-up of the main locations:

- The recent unrest kicked off in Tunisia back in December last year when a young man set himself on fire in protest at the repressive policies of Zine el Abidine ben Ali, president for the past 24 years. At first the military tried to suppress the resulting riots, but later changed tack and removed President ben Ali. It has been subsequently reported that huge quantities of jewellery and cash in various foreign currencies have been found in the former presidential palace.

- Protests in Algeria have so far been less successful, having been 'quelled' by riot police operating under the state of emergency that has, apparently, been in force since 1992! The country has been ruled for eleven years by President Abdelaziz Bouteflika, 'elected' in 1999 with the aid of the military and a fraudulent vote.

- Jordan was pretty much a British puppet until after the Second World War. Since then it has remained a fairly unconstitutional monarchy with a strong military financed by the US, the UK and France. Recent protests in February and March were forcibly dispersed, and protestors severely beaten, if we are to believe reports.

- Oman's head of state is a hereditary sultan, currently Qaboos bin Said al Said, who has led the country since overthrowing his father in 1970 (interesting interpretation of 'hereditary'). The sultan appoints ministers. There have been popular protests this year, but recently they have been broken up with increasing violence.

- Yemen has been ruled by President Ali Abdullah Saleh for 32 years since he more or less assumed power after the assassination of the previous president, Ahmed bin Hussein al-Ghashmi. According to *Wikipedia* (quoting other sources), *'almost half of the population of Yemen live on $2 or less a day, and one-third suffer from chronic hunger. Yemen ranks 146th in the Transparency International 2010 Corruption Perceptions Index, and 15th in the 2010 Failed States Index'*. Protests have continued through February and

March and pro-Saleh forces have been using increasing force to suppress them[34].

- Hosni Mubarak, essentially a dictator installed in 1981 after a military assassination of Anwar el Sadat, ruled Egypt for thirty years until obliged to resign after the armed forces decided to stop supporting him in the face of a popular uprising. According to a recent *Time* article, *'US taxpayers [had been] spending $3.5 million a day on the Egyptian military, buying it everything from F-16 jets to M-1 tanks'*[35] – helping to make it the world's 10th largest military. Sometimes it's hard to tell exactly whose side we're on.

- Problems in Lebanon seem to come down to religion rather than popular unrest. Since the French moved out at the end of World War Two, the country has been governed by an interesting system of power-sharing among the Maronite Christians, Sunni and Shi'i Muslims. It's not easy to understand exactly what's going on in Lebanon these days except that the Shia militant Hezbollah group have been steadily gaining power, and are suspected of having had a hand in the assassination of the Western-backed Prime Minister, Rafik Hariri, in 2005.

- Kuwait is said to have the world's fifth largest oil reserves, and to be its 11th richest country, on a per capita basis. It claims to be a constitutional monarchy, but the 'constitution' seems to consider the hereditary emir to have pretty much absolute power over his subjects. There have been street protests recently, but not much outside support is likely. You may remember George Bush Snr disinterestedly stepping in to rescue little old Kuwait from that big bully, Saddam, back in 1991.

- Lucky little Bahrain, with a total population of just over one million, has the good (or bad) fortune to be rich in oil and pearls. Since 1970, when the British moved out, it has been an absolute monarchy. The present King, Shaikh Hamad bin Isa Al Khalifa, has been on the throne for eleven years. Recent street protests

---

[34] http://en.wikipedia.org/wiki/2011_Yemeni_protests
[35] *Time Magazine*, 14 Feb 2011

demanding rights and freedoms have been 'brutally' put down. Again, we're unlikely to see much Western assistance for the downtrodden masses, given that the incumbent monarch very kindly allows the United States Fifth Fleet to operate from his nation's waters.

- Well, Libya, of course, is another matter. Muammar Gaddafi has been president since leading a military coup in 1969 to oust the monarch, King Idris. You wouldn't expect to find him on any Western leader's list of people to invite to his/her birthday party. President Reagan sent in the US Air Force in 1986, in an unsuccessful attempt to take Gaddafi out. Twenty-five years later, we have a similar scenario, though the US have been hanging back a little and allowing the French to lead the way with their Mirages. Libya, incidentally, has the world's 10th largest proven oil reserves. Interestingly, France and Italy (another participant in the bombing) are its two biggest customers.

- Morocco is another 'constitutional' monarchy whose king, Mohammed VI has wielded fairly all-encompassing powers since ascending the throne in 1956. Parliamentary elections are periodically held, but clearly the public don't feel very represented. Recent protests have been snuffed out by firm police action.

- Pro-democracy campaigners in Saudi Arabia have been largely discouraged from venting their rage by shows of strength from security forces. King Abdullah is not known as the most enlightened of monarchs, and Amnesty International regularly express serious concerns about his commitment to upholding human rights. The CIA website[36] has this to say:

'Saudi Arabia is a destination country for workers from South and Southeast Asia who are subjected to conditions that constitute involuntary servitude including being subjected to physical and sexual abuse, non-payment of wages, confinement, and withholding of passports as a restriction on their movement; domestic workers are particularly vulnerable because some are confined to the house in which they work, unable to seek help; Saudi

---

[36] https://www.cia.gov/library/publications/the-world-factbook/geos/sa.html

Arabia is also a destination country for Nigerian, Yemeni, Pakistani, Afghan, Somali, Malian, and Sudanese children trafficked for forced begging and involuntary servitude as street vendors; some Nigerian women were reportedly trafficked into Saudi Arabia for commercial sexual exploitation.'

Clearly, you are less likely to be held internationally accountable for such activities if you have the world's largest oil reserves. One might be more likely to accept President Obama's concern for human welfare in Libya if his government hadn't recently agreed to sell $60 billion worth of high tech weaponry to the Saudis – said to be the largest arms deal in history. Interestingly, 23 percent of Saudi Arabia's population consists of foreign nationals, yet no one seems to be advising or assisting them to leave.

So what do you get from all that? I'm not sure that I want to draw any sweeping conclusions, except to note that, as I suggested above, the situation is deeply complicated. It is probably safe to say, however, that support for the rise of democracy and the recognition of human rights in the Islamic world are not the major priorities of governments in the United States and the European Union.

'But what about Turkey?' I have been asked. 'Aren't you worried that this revolutionary fervour may spread in that direction?' Well, frankly, I'm not, and I'd like to tell you why.

Let's begin with the nature of government in Turkey in comparison with those countries listed above. The modern Republic of Turkey was born in 1923 from the ashes of the Ottoman Empire. The last hereditary Ottoman sultan had, the previous year, seen the writing on the wall and allowed himself to be whisked away to safety on a British battleship, HMS *Malaya*. At that time, Istanbul had been occupied by the British and their Allies since the end of the First World War, and Sultan Mehmet VI Vahdettin had become their puppet. Turkey was not yet a democracy, but it had definitely asserted its independence, in the face of Allied attempts to subdue and dismember it – and the monarchy had become a relic of the past.

The first true multiparty election was held in Turkey in 1950. It seemed to pass largely unheralded, as far as I am aware, but 2010 marked the 60th anniversary of that moderately significant event. Why it went uncelebrated is open to conjecture. I can think of two possible reasons.

The first is that Turks were probably reluctant to accept that the father of their Republic, Mustafa Kemal Atatürk, had ruled as head of state for fifteen years without troubling himself to hold an election. The second reason may be that, in 1960, 1971 and 1980, the Turkish military intervened in civilian politics and ousted elected governments, so the 60-year period has not been without its hiccups. Nevertheless, those periods of military government were brief, and the reins of power were quickly passed back into elected civilian hands.

Sixty years is quite a significant time span, in global terms, as is the 87 years that have elapsed since the founding of the republic. France is currently into its fifth republic, and had hosted one revolution, two empires, one restoration of the monarchy and the establishment of an alternative monarchy within its first sixty years. The United States republic was still enslaving a large portion of its population eighty years after its foundation, fought a vicious and bloody civil war after ninety years, and was continuing to ethnically cleanse its indigenous peoples after a hundred.

When considering the state of democracy in Turkey, we tend to forget that several important members of the European Union have worse records. Spain, for example, was ruled by a military dictatorship for most of the years from 1923 to 1975, and did not become a democracy until 1978. Portugal managed the feat two years earlier in 1976, after a left-wing military coup in 1974 had ousted the right-wing dictatorship that had been trying to maintain the anachronistic colonial empire. Greece's seven-year military dictatorship collapsed in 1974, interestingly, in the face of a threat of war with Turkey. The junta strongman, Brigadier Ioannides had sponsored the military coup in Cyprus that led to Turkish intervention on the island, and his supporters deserted him as a result. So it could be argued that Greeks should thank Turkey for the re-establishment of democracy in the land that claims it as its home.

Of course, mature democracies understandably view military coups as undesirable, and inconsistent with the ideal of government of, by and for the people. Clearly it didn't do Turkey's claims for international recognition much good to have three such events in the space of twenty years. What those mature democracies may fail to understand is that (paradox though it may seem) the military in Turkey was constitutionally entrusted with the responsibility of maintaining democracy. The threat of militant Islam is very real in this part of the world, and fear of it, very deep-seated in the hearts of secular republicans. The present government in Turkey has been gradually working to curb the power of the military to interfere in political affairs – and has come under a deal of criticism for doing so.

Another positive development in recent years has been the phenomenon known in Turkish as 'açılım', or 'opening-up'. Turkey has long been criticised by Europe for human rights abuses, mistreatment of minorities, and curbing the freedom of the press and the right to protest. Few would argue that Scandinavian levels of personal freedom have been attained – but at least the 'opening-up' has allowed discussion to begin on issues such as the Kurdish situation and relations with Armenians. The Turkish film industry has flourished in the past fifteen years and formerly taboo subjects such as the on-going war in the east, the treatment of villagers, and civil rights abuses under the military regimes, have begun to reach the mass market.

In the end, of course, there's nothing like money to stop people complaining about their lot in life – and clearly much of the unhappiness in those North African and Middle Eastern states is related to perceived disparities in wealth and opportunity. Certainly, Turkey is no paradigm for egalitarian wealth distribution, but average incomes are on the rise, and there is a rapidly growing middle class with real discretionary purchasing power. Per capita GDP increased by 34 percent in the first decade of this century, while inflation fell from an astronomical and chronic seventy percent to an acceptable seven. The process of urbanisation is continuing, and this, combined with rapid population growth, has, of course, created problems. Both rates are now decreasing, however, and this should lead to greater stability and rising standards of living across the board.

Ironically, it may be said that one of Turkey's blessings is a lack of indigenous fossil fuel resources. If a generalisation can be drawn from its neighbours in the region, oil riches can bring disadvantages. Too much wealth can attract unwelcome attention from outsiders, and have a negative affect on the character of its possessors. Despite its lack of oil, Turkey has a larger and more healthily diverse economy than any of its Muslim brother states. Lists compiled by the IMF, the World Bank and the CIA give it a global ranking of 17th, ahead of Indonesia (with four times the population) and the oil-rich Saudis.

Undoubtedly there will be those who say I am painting an unduly rosy picture of a state that still has some way to go to reach the living standards and personal freedoms of the best of the Western nations. There are social and economic injustices in Turkey, and a crying need for more equitable access to education. Turkey has the misfortune to be emerging from its sometimes murky past at a time when Western nations themselves are struggling to maintain the living standards, freedoms and equality they may once have taken for granted. Nevertheless, these days you are less likely to hear Turkey ranked with the Islamic states of the world, and more likely to hear it mentioned in the same sentence as China, India and Brazil.

26

Alone on the World Stage - Turkey's Foreign Policy

6 May 2011

I read an interesting article in a recent issue of *'Time'* magazine. It was entitled 'How Syria and Libya got to be Turkey's Headaches'[37]. It interested me on two counts - first, because it contradicted my own feelings about how events in the Arab world would affect Turkey; and second, because it was written by a Turk who seemed to be portraying her country in an unnecessarily pessimistic light in an international news magazine.

The writer, Pelin Turgut, began by announcing that, with the current crisis in Syria, the *Arab Spring* [had] *arrived on Turkey's doorstep.'* What do you take from that? It seemed to me an unfortunate statement, pandering, as it does, to misinformed Western stereotypes of Turkey. Turks are not Arabs. Unlike the Arab nations experiencing popular unrest, Turkey has a democratically elected parliament and government. Further, there has been no sign of the kind of grass roots protests that have racked neighbouring states. Ms Turgut knows these things, yet she seemed to be implying something different.

---

[37] *'Time'*, April 30 2011

In her article, Ms Turgut seemed to compile a litany of innuendo aimed at discrediting the Turkish Government, with little solid foundation. She called the government of Prime Minister Recep Tayyip Erdoğan 'Islamic-rooted'. What does that mean? Turkey's population is overwhelmingly Muslim, and any government that does not at least pay lip service to that fact has no chance of success at the polls. For nine years I have heard 'secular' Turks claim that Mr Erdoğan's party has a secret agenda to dismantle the secular state and introduce shariah law. If that is the case, they are showing remarkable stealth and patience.

Ms Turgut went on to suggest, with weasel words, that the Turkish government has forsaken attempts to join the European Union, and instead, moved closer to Islamic Arab states. She highlighted Mr Erdoğan's criticism of Israel, and seemed to imply that his government's bridge-building with Syria and Libya were in some way, a bad thing. In fact, as I read it, world opinion has been shifting against Israel's intransigence in the West Bank. It is Israel who is defying the United Nations, not the Turkish government. Similarly, it is the European Union that, rightly or wrongly, has been rejecting Turkey's attempts to gain membership for fifty years – not the other way around. It is hard to imagine that anyone in the USA or Europe would have been happy to see Turkey and Syria go to war – yet Pelin Turgut seemed to be implying some kind of hypocrisy in Turkey's peaceful overtures under Mr Erdoğan's leadership.

Similarly, she criticized what she seemed to see as inconsistency in Turkey's attitude to neighbours experiencing the 'Arab Spring.' She noted that the Turkish PM 'denounced' Mubarak's regime in Egypt, while remaining silent on Libya and Syria - ignoring the fact that the Turkish PM got it right with Egypt, and the jury is still out on Libya. Turks have to live in this part of the world. They don't have the luxury of two thousand kilometres of Europe and five thousand kilometres of Atlantic Ocean buffering them against the realities of the Middle East, so it's hardly surprising that they are less than enthusiastic about charging into neighbouring nations with guns blazing.

Ms Turgut enlisted the support of a couple of 'Turkey experts', Soli Özel, 'international relations professor at Bilgi University and a political columnist', and Henri Barkey who apparently wrote 'an article for the Carnegie Endowment for Peace'. With all due respect to these gentlemen, despite Turkey's increasing interest in playing a peacekeeping and mediating role in the Middle East, it has no power to, and probably no desire to coerce neighbours to follow its wishes. The 'neo-Ottoman' label may have a catchy ring to Turkey's detractors, but on examination, it is a largely meaningless tag. The Ottomans were a religion-centred, autocratic, monarchic empire. The modern Turkish republic is none of these things. However, should a lack of power to enforce its wishes prevent Turkey from attempting a moderating role in the region? Surely no one with a genuine interest in world peace would argue so.

As an example of failed policies, Pelin Turgut cited the presence of Turkish construction companies and workers in Libya. Admittedly, the Turkish government had to evacuate large numbers of its citizens from that troubled nation – but one could argue that sending builders to construct projects is preferable to sending bombers and cruise missiles to destroy them. How many soldiers does the US have in Iraq and Afghanistan? And has their presence there been more successful than the Turkish presence in Libya? Henri Barkey was quoted as criticizing Turkey for having become 'a status quo power' in the region. That may be a little unfair, given Erdoğan's reprimands of Israel and Egypt's Mubarak, and the United States' record arms sale to Saudi Arabia, and its major financial contributions to Mubarak's military machine. In the end, a nation's foreign policy is its own affair – and who is to say that Turkey's foreign policy is any more self-serving than that of the United States or France?

Soli Özel, the international relations expert from Bilgi University asserted, almost gleefully, that "Turkey now finds itself very alone on the world stage." It may be so, but who is to blame? Turkey will never be truly accepted by the Arab Islamic countries, because Turks are not Arabs, and they espouse secular democratic ideals. By its very existence, Turkey is a threat to its autocratic Arab neighbours. On the other hand, it will (most likely) never be fully accepted as one of the Western democracies because it is a Muslim country. Being alone on the world stage is nothing new for Turks. Nevertheless, United Sates foreign policy-makers at least, recognize Turkey's value as a key player on the spot in the volatile but vital Middle East. And Turks themselves, in my opinion, should recognize their need to work together in their isolation.

27

The Price of Progress - Turkey's Economic Miracle

20 May 2011

Turkey's economy is booming. Reputable sources (the World Bank, the IMF and the CIA) rank Turkey as the 15th or 16th largest in the world by GDP, with an annual growth rate of six to eight percent, putting it up there with China and India. The Spanish newspaper 'El Pais' ran an article recently on the Turkish 'Economic Miracle', citing as its chief symbol, the Istanbul Sapphire Tower, currently, at 261 metres, the tallest building in Europe.

In 1973, the Bosporus was spanned by an impressive suspension bridge. In 1988, a second was opened to keep pace with Istanbul's growth. Last year, the go-ahead was given for a third bridge; a rail tube/tunnel is due to open in 2013, linking the Asian and European sides of the city – and plans are currently afoot for a road tunnel. There are 38 universities listed in Istanbul alone, and 74 modern shopping malls, with ten new ones scheduled to open in the next two years.

In April 2011, the Turkish Prime Minister, Recep Tayyip Erdoğan, announced the grandest project yet – a proposed fifty kilometre canal linking the Sea of Marmara and the Black Sea, allowing much of the tanker and container ship traffic that currently passes through the centre of the city, to bypass the Bosporus Strait. PM Erdoğan has attracted a fair amount of flak locally for his 'crazy and magnificent' scheme, but, in fact, it looks like a modest proposal when measured against the Grand Canal of China, completed in 609 CE, and reputed to measure 1794 kilometres in length! Nevertheless, if it comes to fruition, the Istanbul canal will not be much inferior in scale to the Suez or Panama waterways.

This exponential growth is not confined to Istanbul alone. The former imperial capital is, of course, by far the country's largest urban area, with an estimated population of over thirteen million. However, there are at least eight other cities exceeding the one million mark. A month or so ago, I was in Konya for a conference. I had been there twelve years previously when it was a rather sleepy central Anatolian city best known for its Seljuk architecture and as a place of pilgrimage for those visiting the tomb of Mevlana Rumi. On my latest visit, the view from my hotel window was dominated by a 42-storey office tower rising from the opposite side of the street – this in Turkey's seventh largest city.

Number Eight on the list is Antalya, on the Mediterranean coast, which I also had the pleasure of visiting recently. Antalya, the ancient Greek city of Attalia, is one of the jewels on what is sometimes referred to as the Turkish Riviera. We EFL teachers were treated to three nights at the Vogue Avantgarde, a 5-star establishment near the village of Göynük. A sign at reception announced the price of a single room as $450, with a reduction to $660 if you could find someone to share a double. I doubt if any of the guests, we or the Russian tourists, were actually paying that much, but it was a pretty nice place, with multilingual staff, its own beach plus several swimming pools, entertainment on tap, and food that wouldn't have disappointed the guests at Kate and William's wedding.

Now I couldn't begin to guess how many similar palaces of hospitality line Turkey's 4300 kilometres of Mediterranean and Aegean coastline – and no doubt it must still be possible to find a relatively unspoiled beach. Nevertheless, it's becoming increasingly difficult, and this entry in a recent edition of 'Lonely Planet Turkey' for the resort of Ölüdeniz is representative: *Unfortunately, the paradise that many past travellers fondly recall has all but been ruined by the tightly packed belt of hotels behind the beach. [This] used to be one of the highlights of independent travel in Turkey but the development of identical air-conditioned hotels, loud bars and over-priced restaurants has hardly bolstered its appeal.'*

Some friends of mine from Istanbul moved down south to Antalya a few years ago to build their dream house in a village somewhere out of town amidst the orange groves, with views of the Taurus Mountains. Most of us have dreams, but not many of us get to fulfil them, so I hope Andy and Burcu (not their real names) will forgive my mentioning them here. They have a beautiful place to live, and we denizens of megalopolitan Istanbul can only envy them, and hope that the urban sprawl of Antalya will leave them in peace.

Some 300 kilometres to the east of Antalya, citizens of another important Turkish city are bracing for the approach of a different aspect of modernity. Mersin is another urban centre approaching the magic one million population, Turkey's largest port, and proud possessor of a 52-story tower, the nation's tallest when it was built in 1987. A hundred kilometres down the road from Mersin is the town of Akkuyu, where Turkey's first nuclear power plant for the generation of electricity will be built by the Russian state nuclear company Rosatom. Some folks may find it a little strange that Turkey, a notoriously seismically unstable land, is going ahead with a nuclear power station at a time when Japan is struggling to contain the fallout from its crippled plant at Fukushima, damaged by the tsunami in the aftermath of the March earthquake. Nevertheless, Akkuyu is only one of two sites that the Turkish government has earmarked for nuclear-powered electricity generation – the second being at Sinop on the Black Sea coast.

Some may also question Turkey's wisdom in entrusting the building of these facilities to a Russian company. 1986 is fading from living memory, and becoming ancient history, but Turks have good cause to remember the Soviet-era nuclear disaster at Chernobyl in nearby Ukraine. Perhaps the effects of the radiation leakage are less immediate these days. However, the Russian government is currently engaged in building a huge concrete shield to cover the still threatening Chernobyl plant. An expert was asked how long the site would remain a danger. His answer? Around 20,000 years!

Well, Turkey needs energy, there's no questioning that. The country's GDP may exceed that of Saudi Arabia, but it does not possess the oil riches that bless (or curse) its neighbouring guardian of the holy cities of Islam. Turkey is rich in water, a resource arguably more beneficial in the long-term than oil. The GAP project, harnessing the headwaters of the Tigris and Euphrates rivers includes the world's fourth largest dam. However, the rising waters will soon cover the ancient city of Zeugma, location of some of the most magnificent mosaics of the ancient world. Highlighting the paradoxical truth that a blessing can also be a curse, Turkey's treasury of historical riches adds hugely to the cost of every development project. The Istanbul Metro system is several years behind schedule, and no doubt considerably over budget because excavations constantly turn up remains of Greek and Roman temples, harbours, churches and cemeteries, which demand the attentions of armies of archaeologists before construction can continue. A bridge which will carry the Metro trains over the Golden Horn has had to be redesigned several times to comply with UNESCO demands that it must not blight the domed and minaretted skyline of ancient Istanbul with incongruous modernity.

Coming back to nuclear power stations - nobody wants to live next door to one, but what can you do? George Bush the Elder is notorious for his refusal to accept the recommendations of the Rio de Janeiro Earth Summit in 1992 with the immortal line: 'The American way of life is non-negotiable.' Back then, perhaps, the danger we face as a planet was not so clear, at least not to the GOP and its supporters. Now that China, with its 1.3 billion population, has overtaken Japan as the world's second largest economy, we are starting to get it. What happens when those rising Chinese middle classes are able to afford the 'American way of life' to which they probably aspire? And then there's India, picked to succeed China as the most populous nation by 2025. I don't know their figures, but I can extrapolate from what I know about Turkey, with its comparatively miniscule population of 75 million. Anyone who lives in Istanbul will tell you about the nightmare traffic in the city - yet the proportion of motor vehicles per capita in Turkey is less than 25 percent. What will happen when that figure approaches the Western norm of 70 to 80 percent? Then do the maths for India and China. Then give some thought to getting rid of the SUV, and installing a solar water heater and a wind-powered generator on your rooftop.

28

Neo-Ottomanism: A new direction for Turkey?

18 June 2011

O nce upon a time I dabbled a little in politics, to the extent that I actually tried twice to get myself elected as a Member of Parliament. It was a great experience and I'm glad I did it. I guess my main motivation was to preserve my right to criticize. People would say, 'Well, if you're so smart, why don't you do something constructive to change things?' I wasn't successful, of course, and I'm equally glad, in retrospect, that I wasn't. To get elected on a party ticket you have to juggle the dictates of the party itself, the fickle winds of public opinion, the oppressive power of the media circus, your own desire for power, and your private beliefs and personal integrity. All too often, the still small voice of the latter is drowned by the insistent bellowing of the former.

All politicians know this, of course, and choose to pay the price for success, so you can't feel too sorry for them. Barack Obama should have known (if he truly didn't) before swearing the presidential oath, that the Pentagon wouldn't allow him to shut down Guantanamo and stop the torture; that adhering to the demands of the Armenian diaspora would run him into difficulties with the Turkish Government; and that the too-big-to-fail US banking sector would force him to help them out of their self-dug hole with a multi-billion dollar taxpayer-funded handout. Democracy is the machinery that allows us to call politicians to account when they stray too far from the path we want them to follow. Never fear, America, here comes Mitt Romney to the rescue!

I guess have a longish history as a political sceptic, but I do feel a certain sympathy for those charged with the responsibility of forming Turkey's foreign policy these days. Neo-Ottomanism is a word I hear bandied around a lot. The implication seems to be that Turkey is moving away from the Western orientation it has followed since the founding of the republic, turning instead towards the Central Asian and Middle Eastern regions associated with its Turkic and Ottoman origins. The argument clearly has appeal for those, abroad and at home, wishing to label Turkey as eastern, Islamic, uncivilized and 'other'; and the present government as all those things, plus backward-looking and anti-democratic. What do I think? Let me share my thoughts ...

The Turkish Republic had its birth in a land devastated by decades of war – and it has often been said that the first casualty of war is truth. The Ottoman Empire had been reduced by a century of nationalist splintering from within, and imperialist manipulation from without, to a shrunken rump on the verge of collapse. The last nationalist movement to emerge was Turkish nationalism, forced into self-awareness by the threat of imminent destruction. In order to foster this national identity, the leaders of the republican independence movement were obliged to create an identity of Turkishness, to decimate the elitist Ottoman language and exalt its poor Turkish relation; to develop myths of a legendary Turkish past, and sever ties to the Islamic Empire which had finally been brought to its knees by Western European power.

The new Republic had, from its inception, an uncomfortable relationship with the Ottoman Empire from which it sprang. Osman Gazi, the founder of the Ottoman state, was a 13th century Turkish warlord. The Ottoman Sultans, for centuries, claimed, largely by dint of military might, the title of Caliph, or leader of the Muslim 'nation'. Nevertheless, though officially Muslim, the empire contained relatively autonomous populations of Jews and Christians, as well as the various Islamic communities. The Ottomans did not regard themselves as 'Turkish'. Turks were the warriors and tillers of the soil. The basis of the Ottoman language may have been Turkish, but it had substantial overlays of Arabic and Persian, incorporating three distinct language families[38]. The Ottomans were a ruling elite intermarrying with Russian and Greek princesses, and happily mingling with maidens fair from the conquered lands of Europe. In its declining years, however, their Empire had become a virtual puppet of the European Great Powers, accepting support and indignities from all and sundry to eke out its existence a little longer. When the armed forces of France and Britain occupied Istanbul at the end of the First World War, the 'virtual' puppet status became reality. The Sultan and his ministers were compelled to sign at Sevres a treaty that would have dismembered the once mighty empire. The final insult must have been the Entente-sponsored invasion of Anatolia by the army of Greece, intent on re-establishing its ancient Byzantine glory.

In short, we can say that the founders of the Turkish Republic had to split from and deny pretty much everything that the Ottoman Empire had represented. The fostering of a Turkish national identity required a rejection of all things Ottoman, even religion – yet the new state, unlike its predecessor, was now almost exclusively Muslim. Contradictions abounded, so, of necessity, there was some rewriting of history, some adjusting of reality, some myth-creation in order to ensure the survival of a nation that, like Hans Andersen's ugly duckling, no one else in the world really wanted.

It is only recently that Turks have started to become comfortable with their Ottoman heritage. Sufficient time has passed that they can begin to feel pride in the achievements of ancestors whose existence cannot be denied. Most of the excesses of early republican nationalism and secularism are being quietly put away on high shelves. Atatürk himself insisted that the ezan, the Muslim call to prayer, should be intoned in Turkish. Now that is a dead issue. Even the most ardent Kemalists seem content to hear Arabic broadcast at high volume five times (or more) a day from a forest of increasingly lofty minarets. One of the most popular drama series on television these days is "Muhteşem Yüzyıl" ("The Magnificent Century"), set in the 1500s, during the reign of Sultan Suleiman, generally acknowledged to have presided over the Ottoman Empire at the zenith of its power. Modern Turkey is achieving a synthesis, as its middle class multiplies and the process of urbanization

---

[38] English, in comparison, though indebted to several major sources, is pretty pure Indo-European.

accelerates, of modernity, economic consumption, globalization, secular democratic government, Islamic traditions and Turkishness. That is as it should be. The government may try to direct these processes but it cannot control them.

So far, then, I have been looking at the domestic situation in Turkey, but of course, there is another aspect to the label of Neo-Ottomanism. When the Turkish Republic came into being, its founders resolved to turn towards the West in the search for a new direction. The founding principles included democratic republicanism, separation of religion and government, state-sponsored economic development, and reforms of alphabet, language, clothing and religious practices. Europe represented the goals of the new republic, and all things Western and European became desirable. Although remaining neutral during the Second World War, Turkey sent armed forces to the Korean conflict, and was a major military contributor to NATO defences during the Cold War. I have recently learned that, when President JF Kennedy was indignantly ordering the Soviets to withdraw their missiles from Cuba, the United States had bases in Turkey with missiles trained on the USSR. I'm sure the Soviets knew about these, were not too happy about them, and very likely had Turkish locations pretty high on their list of targets to hit, should the need arise. It was a risk the Turkish Government took, one assumes out of a desire for friendship with the West.

At this point, I would like to quote from *Wikipedia* on the subject of Turkey's attempts to gain admission to the European Union. I am aware that some people disparage *Wikipedia* as a source, but on this one I'm prepared to trust them. You can check the facts elsewhere if you have the time and the inclination:

'*Turkey's application to accede to the European Union was made on 14 April 1987. Turkey has been an associate member of the European Union (EU) and its predecessors since 1963. After the ten founding members, Turkey was one of the first countries to become a member of the Council of Europe in 1949, and was also a founding member of the Organisation for Economic Co-operation and Development (OECD) in 1961 and the Organization for Security and Co-operation in Europe (OSCE) in 1973. The country has also been an associate member of the Western European Union since 1992, and is a part of the "Western Europe" branch of the*

Western European and Others Group (WEOG) at the United Nations. Turkey signed a Customs Union agreement with the EU in 1995 and was officially recognised as a candidate for full membership on 12 December 1999, at the Helsinki summit of the European Council. Negotiations were started on 3 October 2005, and the process, should it be in Turkey's favour, is likely to take at least a decade to complete. The membership bid has become a major controversy of the ongoing enlargement of the European Union.[39]

It looks to me as though Turkey has been pretty determined, one might say patient, in its efforts to be accepted into the European fold. I am well aware of the arguments against acceptance, however, spoken and unspoken, and (just between you and me) I suspect that a blue moon will rise over a cold day in hell when the EU finally welcomes Turkey aboard as a full member. So what are the Turks to do in the mean time?

The key issue that makes Europeans shy away from inviting Turkey into their club, namely religion, is the very factor that gives Turks an advantage when it comes to dealing with nations in the Middle East and Central Asia. Muslims have felt marginalized by Western societies for a long time now, and the accelerating speed of modernization has served to accentuate the sense of superiority in the West, and corresponding sense of exclusion in the rest of the world. Turkey, with its unique combination of secular democracy and traditional Islamic viewpoint, coupled with the detachment that its Turkishness brings to the mix, finds itself in a position to play a mediating role in an area that remains a mystery to most in the West. Central Asian Turkic republics, freeing themselves from decades of oppression by Russian and Soviet conquerors, see Turkey as the big brother that has trodden the difficult path they themselves aspire to follow. Middle Eastern states have a more problematic relationship with their liberal neighbour, but still, Turkey stands as an example of a country that has managed to achieve impressive political, social and economic freedoms while retaining its Islamic identity.

Is it any wonder, then, that the government of Turkey, and the private sector of its own accord, have been working to build bridges with neighbouring states in their immediate vicinity and further to the east?

---

[39] http://en.wikipedia.org/wiki/Accession_of_Turkey_to_the_European_Union

Can Western nations continue dangling carrots while holding Turkey at arm's length, and at the same time, seriously expect the Turks to forego all other international contact in the hopes of future acceptance? The United States at least, has a pragmatic approach – unlike France for example, they refrain from grandstanding to special interest groups at home who have a historical axe to grind. They encourage EU members to adopt a more positive approach to Turkey's membership application – even if only because of Turkey's strategic geo-political significance. Britain also pushes Turkey's case from time to time – though a cynic might suggest this stems more from its desire to maintain a Euro-sceptic position than from any great love for Turks as a race.

In the mean time, we see Turkish construction companies working in partnership with locals in Kazakhstan and Libya, and Turkish educational foundations building schools. We have seen the Turkish government (in league with Brazil) trying its own approach to ease international tensions over Iran's nuclear development programme. We are seeing tent cities established near the southeast border to accept thousands of refugees fleeing violence and oppression in neighbouring Syria. Students from 130 nations came to Ankara in 2011 to participate in the 9th International Turkish Language Festival.

In 2010 Istanbul was chosen as one of Europe's Capitals of Culture, and, major projects were carried out all over the city to showcase its historical riches. Twenty-one million Turkish Liras were spent on a three-year restoration of the 16th century Süleimaniye Mosque, simply the best of many architectural treasures built during the reign of that 'Magnificent' sultan. But it is not merely Istanbul and Ottoman treasures that demand huge sums for historical restoration and preservation. A farmer near the Black Sea city of Zonguldak, better known for its coal mines, recently uncovered, while digging foundations for a hothouse on his property, the perfectly preserved mosaic floor of a 3rd century Roman villa[40].

Then there are the Ottoman heritage buildings beyond the boundaries of modern Turkey. The international community recognises the debt owed to the civilisations of Ancient Greece and Rome, and there is no difficulty in raising money to restore and preserve classical remains, wherever they may be located today. The British Empire left its archi-

---

[40] 'Hürriyet' newspaper: http://www.hurriyet.com.tr/gundem/16253467.asp

tectural footprint all over the world, from Sydney to Kolkata, Istanbul to Shanghai. Most of those cities are in countries that have long-since thrown off the colonial yoke, yet they are happy to find new uses for the buildings. The Ottoman heritage is a different matter. In the Balkans and Greece, emergent Christian states couldn't wait to erase all traces of their Muslim Ottoman past. In Central Asia, a century or two of Russian and Soviet hegemony, and economies with little surplus for luxuries, have combined to the detriment of important historical sites. Recently the Turkish Government has been involving itself in the restoration of their historical heritage in neighbouring nations. There are critics who see this as yet another aspect of emerging Neo-Ottomanism. Yet imagine the outcry if Turkey allowed, never mind contributed to, the decay and destruction of a 15th century church or cathedral within its borders. Without Turkish Government involvement, the six-century-old Fethiye Mosque in Athens would continue its descent into rubble; the Orhun inscriptions in Mongolia, the oldest known written documents of Turkic history, would meet the same fate, as would, probably, the madrasah where Mevlana Jelaleddin Rumi was born in Afghanistan[41].

As I said in my opening paragraphs, I don't generally have much sympathy for politicians. Dealing with criticism is part of their job, as are making unfulfillable promises and obfuscating the truth. Nevertheless, I can't help feeling that the present Turkish government gets more than its fair share of unreasonable criticism. Can they really be in the United States' pocket, and at the same time, have a shariah and Neo-Ottoman expansionist agenda? Should they spend taxpayer money restoring and caring for their historic buildings, or leave them to rot and decay – and if restoration is the decision, who should decide which ones and where? Should Turkey cut itself off from contact with its Muslim and Central Asian neighbours in the hopes of currying favour with Europe? The path of political success is a minefield, and I'm pleased, when I look back, that New Zealand voters kept me from it.

---

[41] 'Today's Zaman' newspaper: http://www.todayszaman.com/news-246215-turkey-takes-care-of-ottoman-legacy-abroad.html

29

Gay Rights and Syrian refugees

5 July 2011

There was a big Gay Pride march in Istanbul at the end of June. I have to tell you right out that I didn't participate. In fact, to my shame, I didn't even take a lot of interest in the event, so what I'm about to share with you was gleaned from a retrospective reading of the CNN report:

> 'Activists say the annual Turkish Gay Pride Parade, now in its ninth year, is the only march of its kind in a majority-Muslim country. Several thousand supporters of lesbian, gay, bisexual and transgender rights carried signs and rainbow flags as they made their way down one of Istanbul's busiest pedestrian thoroughfares.'[42]

Now the reason I'm telling you this is that I read a news item around the same time summarising a report released by the human rights group, Amnesty International. The headline read 'Amnesty report condemns

---

[42] CNN news: http://www.cnn.com/2011/WORLD/meast/06/26/turkey.gay.pride/index .html

Turkey's gay rights laws.' Well, I didn't know much about the details of Turkey's laws in this area, so the article inspired me to do a little research, and here are some of my findings:

- Same-sex sexual activity is illegal in the following countries: Kuwait, Lebanon, Oman, Qatar, Saudi Arabia, Syria, the United Arab Emirates, Yemen, Afghanistan, Bangladesh, Bhutan, Iran, Pakistan, Malaysia, Samoa, Jamaica, Barbados, Algeria, Libya, Egypt and Morocco.

- It is legal for women, but illegal for males, in Singapore, the Cook Islands and Tonga.

- In Malaysia, Saudi Arabia, and the United Arab Emirates (which includes Dubai), offenders can be punished by fines, a prison sentence, or whipping. Practising gays in Jamaica can be sentenced to ten years imprisonment with hard labour.

- In Turkey, on the other hand, it has been legal since 1858. By comparison, it was legalised for males in New Zealand in 1986, and in Australia, as recently as 1994.[43]

I was curious to know what the Amnesty International report had to say about these other countries, some of which are on friendly trading and sporting terms with progressive and enlightened Western nations. Accordingly I googled 'amnesty international gay rights report' and was interested to find that most of the results referred to the report's censuring of Turkey, and none of them even hinted that there might be countries with worse records.

As the CNN report above pointed out, the Istanbul Gay Pride parade is the 'only march of its kind in a majority-Muslim country'. Still, the marchers could have been (and some of them apparently were) protesting about the treatment of gays in Turkey. It's perhaps worth noting, then, that demonstrators from a nearby pro-Kurdish gathering, fleeing from police teargas, found sanctuary among the ranks of the proud gays, who apparently were allowed to proceed with their activities unmolested.

---

[43] http://en.wikipedia.org/wiki/LGBT_rights_by_country_or_territory

Turkish police are not noted for their soft approach to undesirable demonstrations, yet the gay marchers were permitted to exhibit their pride without let or hindrance.

Still, you will say, turning a blind eye to one brief march on one day of the year doesn't necessarily prove that the Turkish authorities show the same tolerance all year round, and I agree with you – so I looked further. I checked out the tourist scene, and I turned up a website calling itself 'Pink News'. Under a header announcing 'Turkish Delights', the travel writer had this to say: *'Fancy a break that offers more than a week in an average hotel or a whirlwind city guidebook tour of your destination? If you're looking for a holiday that's far from the madding crowd or something with a slightly different twist, then travel company Journey Anatolia might just have the ideal options for you. Oh, and did we mention that they're all in Turkey? So, chances are you'll need to pack the sunscreen for some beautiful weather.'*[44] Positively gushing, and no mention of whippings or hard labour.

For a second opinion, I turned to my trusty 'Lonely Planet Turkey'[45]. *'The gay scene in Istanbul,'* they said, *'has been characterized as homely rather than raunchy . . . There are an increasing number of openly gay bars and nightclubs in the city . . . Hamams* (Turkish baths) *are a gay fave . . .'* Outside of Istanbul, *'attitudes are changing . . . but there are sporadic reports of violence towards gays – the message is discretion.'*

Aha! 'Violence towards gays!' There it is! However, it seems that such violence is more likely to occur within families than as a result of institutional brutality. Undoubtedly, in certain parts of Turkey, among uneducated villagers, there is still a culture that sees killing as a way of cleansing a family's honour – and this violence is as likely to be directed towards wayward heterosexual young women, as against gays. Of course it is wrong, and Turkey needs to extend civilization and education to all parts of the country before it can expect to be welcomed into the European Union. However, I would like to balance the ledger by offering two points for your consideration.

First, there is a big, wild world out there, and not all of it is exactly as we well-brought up, well educated, open-minded, tolerant, humanitarian fortunates from developed nations might wish it to be. We do well to remember this when we go a-travelling in foreign climes. As 'Lonely

---

[44] http://www.pinknews.co.uk/news/articles/2005-7900.html/
[45] 2007 edition

Planet' clearly warns, 'the message is discretion'. I read recently about a countryman of mine, visiting Papua New Guinea, shot full of arrows and nearly killed by a local tribesman who apparently had taken a fancy to his French girlfriend[46]. I'm not saying I don't sympathise with the poor guy, and his girlfriend, who was reportedly raped at the same time. However, we know that Papua New Guinea is one of the last paradises on Earth for anthropologists keen to see how our less civilised relatives eke out an existence – and the flipside of this is very likely to be a certain unpredictability on the part of natives who may be unaware of the niceties of courting rituals in more civilised circles.

Another compatriot achieved international fame as a yachtsman a few years ago. Sir Peter Blake was knighted by the New Zealand government after setting a circumnavigation record in the Whitbread Round-the-World race, and winning (and defending) the coveted America's Cup in the 1990s. After retiring from yacht racing, Sir Peter was being spoken of as a possible successor to the legendary Jacques Cousteau. Tragically, his boat was attacked, and he was killed, by pirates at the mouth of the Amazon delta while on an environmental exploration trip gathering data for the United Nations. Once again, I'm not intending to show a lack of human sympathy here. I merely want to point out the obvious – that it probably wouldn't have happened if he'd stayed at home in Bayswater, Auckland. Peter Blake knew that too, of course, and he chose to go, knowing the risks.

My second point relates to what some might consider a more immediate human rights issue. During the first weeks of June 2011, refugees were fleeing across the border from Syria into southeast Turkey to escape the violent suppression of protests against President Bashar al-Ashad's regime. Some 15,000 Syrians reportedly crossed into Turkey before Syrian forces closed the border towards the end of the month. Subsequently, reports say, several thousand returned to Syria. The reasons are not totally clear, but it seems men may have brought their families to the sanctuary of Turkey before returning to continue the fight on their own soil. The plight of these refugees was recently given more media attention in the West as a result of a visit by UN goodwill ambassador, Angelina Jolie.

---

[46] TVNZ news: http://tvnz.co.nz/national-news/kiwi-pulls-arrows-his-chest-after-jungle-attack-4274756

Well, as I think I acknowledged above, Turkey, cannot claim a lily-white record on human rights across the board. On the other hand, if the truth be told, few countries can. Perhaps the best we can hope for is a balanced picture, showing our strengths as well as our weaknesses.

www.ingramcontent.com/pod-product-compliance
Lightning Source LLC
Chambersburg PA
CBHW060254290526
45789CB00001B/322